The Complete

Sayings of Jesus

THE COMPLETE SAYINGS OF

Jesus

CHRIST'S OWN WORDS

from THE LIVING BIBLE *Paraphrased*

Arranged in sequence by
ARTHUR HINDS
and prepared in the text of The Living Bible
by the editors of
FCL

Introduction by
NORMAN VINCENT PEALE, D.D.

FOUNDATION FOR CHRISTIAN LIVING

PAWLING, NEW YORK 12564

To
Lunsford P. Yandell
with sincere appreciation
for making this book
possible

Introduction

by Norman Vincent Peale, D.D.

One of the supreme spiritual moments which have enriched my life came the day I read *The Complete Sayings of Jesus*. So fascinated was I that I could not put it down and read it at one sitting. It was a moving and unforgettable experience in which I had the awesome feeling of actually being in the presence of Jesus. Reading His sayings produced a strangely compelling identification with the sights, sounds and atmosphere of those early times, and the Lord's actual presence became profoundly real. When I finished the book I came back to present reality with a start. This amazing affect was created by the fact that in these pages is recorded every word spoken by Jesus and in the sequence in which He uttered His immortal teachings.

This important volume offers an in-depth spiritual experience, one in which the reader follows the Master through the villages and about the lake and into the cities, hearing His priceless comments to individuals and His sermons to vast multitudes. The reading of all of His words at one time and in chronological order produces an effect quite different from that which is attained by reading isolated Scripture passages in which His spoken words appear, as spiritually uplifting as these are. The impact upon mind and heart of His whole message, taken together, is profound.

The book gives a panoramic concept of the thoughts and teachings of Jesus. And so grand and noble is the impression made upon the mind that the reader has an enhanced understanding of the purpose of this, the greatest life ever lived. For spiritual understanding, heartfelt comfort, and soul growth, *The Complete Sayings of Jesus* is unique.

I shall always by grateful that Lunsford P. Yandell made the predecessor volume of this work known to me years ago. He explained that a friend of his, a businessman, Arthur Hinds, sensed the importance of bringing the words of Jesus together in chronological form so that the full sweep and completeness of the immortal message might more effectively be felt and comprehended. These men had a keen and sensitive consciousness of the ineffable power of the words of Jesus and, in a desire to relate them more succinctly to busy modern people, arranged them in this convenient and readable form. The thousands who have read the book, through our recommendation, have reported that it has brought great spiritual blessing to them.

Now Mr. Yandell has generously conveyed the publication rights of *The Complete Sayings of Jesus* to the Foundation for Christian Living. Our editors have, with painstaking and reverent scholarship, taken the material from THE LIVING BIBLE text, with permission of Tyndale House Publishers. I commend this new and attractive edition to all who desire the creative touch of the living Christ upon their lives.

Contents

The Complete

Sayings of Jesus

1 Beginnings

The Greatest of 42 Generations

These are the ancestors of Jesus Christ, a descendant of King David and of Abraham:

Abraham was the father of Isaac; Isaac was the father of . . .

. . . Jesse was the father of King David. David was the father of Solomon; Solomon was the father of . . .

. . . Josiah was the father of Jechoniah and his brothers (born at the time of the exile to Babylon).

Jechoniah was the father of . . .

. . . Jacob was the father of Joseph (who was the husband of Mary, the mother of Jesus Christ the Messiah).

These are fourteen of the generations from Abraham to King David; and fourteen from King David's time to the exile; and fourteen from the exile to Christ.

Matthew 1: 1–2; 6–7; 11–12; 16–17.

Birth of Christ

About this time Caesar Augustus, the Roman Emperor, decreed that a census should be taken throughout the nation.

Everyone was required to return to his ancestral home for this registration. Because Joseph was a member of the royal line, he had to go to Bethlehem in Judea, King David's ancient home—journeying there from the Galilean village of Nazareth. He took with him Mary, his fiancée, who was obviously pregnant by this time.

While they were there, the time came for her baby to be born;

and she gave birth to her first child, a son. She wrapped him in a blanket and laid him in a manger, because there was no room for them in the village inn.

That night some shepherds were in the fields outside the village, guarding their flocks of sheep. Suddenly an angel appeared among them. "Don't be afraid!" he said. "I bring you the most joyful news ever announced, and it is for everyone! The Savior—yes, the Messiah, the Lord—has been born tonight in Bethlehem! You will find a baby wrapped in a blanket, lying in a manger!"

They ran to the village and found their way to Mary and Joseph. And there was the baby, lying in the manger.

Eight days later, at the baby's circumcision ceremony, he was named Jesus, the name given him by the angel before he was even conceived.

Luke 2: 1–12; 16–21.

The Wise Men Come

Jesus was born in the town of Bethlehem, in Judea, during the reign of King Herod.

At about that time some astrologers from eastern lands arrived in Jerusalem, asking, "Where is the newborn King of the Jews? for we have seen his star in far-off eastern lands, and have come to worship him."

King Herod was deeply disturbed by their question. He called a meeting of the Jewish religious leaders.

"Did the prophets tell us where the Messiah would be born?" he asked.

"Yes, in Bethlehem, a Judean village," they said.

Then Herod sent a private message to the astrologers, asking them to come to see him; at this meeting he found out from them the exact time when they first saw the star. Then he told them, "Go to Bethlehem and search for the child. And when you find him, come back and tell me so that I can go and worship him too!"

The astrologers started out again. And look! The star appeared to them again, standing over Bethlehem. Their joy knew no bounds!

Entering the house where the baby and Mary his mother were, they threw themselves down before him, worshiping. Then they opened their presents and gave him gold, frankincense and myrrh. But when they returned to their own land, they didn't go through Jerusalem to report to Herod, for God had warned them in a dream to go home another way.

After they were gone, an angel of the Lord appeared to Joseph in a dream. "Get up and flee to Egypt with the baby and his mother," the angel said, "and stay there until I tell you to return, for King Herod is going to try to kill the child." That same night he left for Egypt with Mary and the baby, and stayed there until King Herod's death.

When Herod died, an angel of the Lord appeared in a dream to Joseph in Egypt, and told him, "Get up and take the baby and his mother back to Israel."

So he returned immediately to Israel with Jesus and his mother. But on the way he was frightened to learn that the new king was Herod's son, Archelaus. Then, in another dream, he was warned not to go to Judea, so they went to Galilee instead, and lived in Nazareth.

Matthew 2: 1–15; 19–23.

Great Even as a Boy

The child became a strong, robust lad, and was known for wisdom beyond his years; and God poured out his blessings on him.

When Jesus was twelve years old he accompanied his parents to Jerusalem for the annual Passover Festival, which they attended each year. After the celebration was over they started home to Nazareth, but Jesus stayed behind in Jerusalem. His parents didn't miss him the first day, for they assumed he was with friends among the other travelers. But when he didn't show up that evening, they started to look for him among their relatives and friends; and when they couldn't find him, they went back to Jerusalem to search for him there.

Three days later they finally discovered him. He was in the Temple, sitting among the teachers of Law, discussing deep questions with them and amazing everyone with his understanding and answers.

His parents didn't know what to think. "Son!" his mother said to him, "Why have you done this to us? Your father and I have been frantic searching for you everywhere."

"But why did you need to search?" he asked. "Didn't you realize that I would be here at the Temple, in my Father's House?" They didn't understand what he meant.

Then he returned to Nazareth with them and was obedient to them; and his mother stored away all these things in her heart. So Jesus grew both tall and wise, and was loved by God and man.*

Luke 2: 40–52.

Baptized in the Jordan

While they were living in Nazareth, John the Baptist began preaching out in the Judean wilderness. His constant theme was, "Turn from your sins . . . turn to God . . . for the Kingdom of Heaven is coming soon."

Isaiah the prophet had told about John's ministry centuries before! He had written, "I hear a shout from the wilderness, 'Prepare a road for the Lord—straighten out the path where he will walk.' "

John's clothing was woven from camel's hair and he wore a leather belt; his food was locusts and wild honey.

People from Jerusalem and from all over the Jordan Valley, and, in fact, from every section of Judea went out to the wilderness to hear him preach, and when they confessed their sins, he baptized them in the Jordan River.

Then Jesus went from Galilee to the Jordan River to be baptized there by John. John didn't want to do it. "This isn't

*For some reason unknown to us there exists no record of Jesus' life between the age of 12 and the age of 30.

16

proper," he said. "I am the one who needs to be baptized by you."

But Jesus said, "Please do it, for I must do all that is right."

So then John baptized him. After his baptism, as soon as Jesus came up out of the water, the heavens were opened to him and he saw the Spirit of God coming down in the form of a dove. And a voice from heaven said, "This is my beloved Son, and I am wonderfully pleased with him."

Jesus was about thirty years old when he began his public ministry.

Matthew 3: 1–6; 13–17; Mark 1: 10–11; Luke 3: 22–23.

Temptation for Earthly Power Rejected

Then Jesus, full of the Holy Spirit, left the Jordan River, being urged by the Spirit out into the barren wastelands of Judea, where Satan tempted him for forty days.

For forty days and forty nights he ate nothing and became very hungry.

Satan said, "If you are God's Son, tell this stone to become a loaf of bread."

But Jesus told him, "No! For the Scriptures tell us that bread won't feed men's souls; obedience to every word of God is what we need."

Then Satan took him to Jerusalem to the roof of the Temple. "Jump off," he said, "and prove you are the Son of God; for the Scriptures declare, 'God will send his angels to keep you from harm,' . . . they will prevent you from smashing on the rocks below."

Jesus retorted, "It also says not to put the Lord your God to a foolish test!"

Satan took him to the peak of a very high mountain and showed him the nations of the world and all their glory.

And the devil told him, "I will give you all these splendid kingdoms and their glory—for they are mine to give to anyone I wish—if you will only get down on your knees and worship me."

"Get out of here, Satan," Jesus told him. "The Scriptures say,

'Worship only the Lord God. Obey only him.' "

Then Satan went away, and angels came and cared for Jesus.

Matthew 4: 2–11; Luke 4: 1–7.

People Begin to Follow Jesus

The Jewish leaders sent priests and assistant priests from Jerusalem to ask John whether he claimed to be the Messiah.

"I am not the Christ," he said.

"Well then, who are you?" they asked.

"I am a voice from the barren wilderness, shouting as Isaiah prophesied, 'Get ready for the coming of the Lord!' "

Then they asked him, "If you aren't the Messiah what right do you have to baptize?"

John told them, "I merely baptize with water, but right here in the crowd is someone you have never met, who will soon begin his ministry among you, and I am not even fit to be his slave."

This incident took place at Bethany, a village on the other side of the Jordan River where John was baptizing.

The next day John saw Jesus coming toward him and said, "Look! There is the Lamb of God who takes away the world's sin! He is the one I was talking about. At the time God sent me to baptize he told me, 'When you see the Holy Spirit descending and resting upon someone—he is the one you are looking for. He is the one who baptizes with the Holy Spirit.' I saw it happen to this man, and I therefore testify that he is the Son of God."

The following day as John was standing with two of his disciples, Jesus walked by. John looked at him intently and then declared, "See! There is the Lamb of God!"

Then John's two disciples turned and followed Jesus.

Jesus looked around and saw them following. "What do you want?" he asked them.

"Sir," they replied, "where do you live?"

"Come and see," he said. They went with him to the place where he was staying and were with him from about four

People Begin to Follow Jesus

o'clock that afternoon until the evening. (One of these men was Andrew, Simon Peter's brother.)

Andrew then went to find his brother Peter and told him, "We have found the Messiah!" And he brought Peter to meet Jesus.

Jesus looked intently at Peter for a moment and then said, "You are Simon, John's son—but you shall be called Peter, the rock!"

The next day Jesus decided to go to Galilee. He found Philip and told him, "Come with me." (Philip was from Bethsaida, Andrew and Peter's home town.)

Philip now went off to look for Nathanael and told him, "We have found the Messiah!—the very person Moses and the prophets told about! His name is Jesus, the son of Joseph from Nazareth!"

"Nazareth!" exclaimed Nathanael. "Can anything good come from there?"

"Just come and see for yourself," Philip declared.

As they approached, Jesus said, "Here comes an honest man —a true son of Israel."

"How do you know what I am like?" Nathanael demanded.

And Jesus replied, "I could see you under the fig tree before Philip found you."

Nathanael replied, "Sir, you are the Son of God—the King of Israel!"

Jesus asked him, "Do you believe all this just because I told you I had seen you under the fig tree? You will see greater proofs than this. You will even see heaven open and the angels of God coming back and forth to me, the Messiah."

John 1: 19–30; 33–51.

2 Power

At the Marriage Feast

Two days later Jesus' mother was a guest at a wedding in the village of Cana in Galilee, and Jesus and his disciples were invited too. The wine supply ran out during the festivities, and Jesus' mother came to him with the problem.

"I can't help you now," he said. "It isn't yet my time for miracles."

But his mother told the servants, "Do whatever he tells you."

Six stone waterpots were standing there; and held perhaps twenty to thirty gallons each. Then Jesus told the servants to fill them to the brim with water. When this was done he said, "Dip some out and take it to the master of ceremonies." The master of ceremonies tasted the water that was now wine.

This miracle at Cana in Galilee was Jesus' first public demonstration of his heaven-sent power. And his disciples believed that he really was the Messiah.

After the wedding he left for Capernaum for a few days with his mother, brothers, and disciples.

Then it was time for the annual Jewish Passover celebration, and Jesus went to Jerusalem.

In the Temple area he saw merchants selling cattle, sheep, and doves for sacrifices, and money changers behind their counters. Jesus made a whip from some ropes and chased them all out, and drove out the sheep and oxen, scattering the money changers' coins over the floor and turning over their tables! Then, going over to the men selling doves, he told them, "Get these things out of here. Don't turn my Father's House into a market!"

"What right have you to order them out?" the Jewish leaders demanded. "If you have this authority from God, show us a miracle to prove it."

"All right," Jesus replied, "this is the miracle I will do for you: Destroy this sanctuary and in three days I will raise it up!"

"What!" they exclaimed. "It took forty-six years to build this Temple, and you can do it in three days?"

But by "this sanctuary" he meant his body.

John 2: 1–21.

The Great Teacher at Work

After dark one night a Jewish religious leader named Nicodemus, a member of the sect of the Pharisees, came for an interview with Jesus. "Sir," he said, "We all know that God has sent you to teach us. Your miracles are proof enough of this."

Jesus replied, "With all the earnestness I possess I tell you this: Unless you are born again, you can never get into the Kingdom of God."

"Born again!" exclaimed Nicodemus. "What do you mean? How can an old man go back into his mother's womb and be born again?"

Jesus replied, "What I am telling you so earnestly is this: Unless one is born of water* and the Spirit, he cannot enter the Kingdom of God. Men can only reproduce human life, but the Holy Spirit gives new life from heaven; so don't be surprised at my statement that you must be born again! Just as you can hear the wind but can't tell where it comes from or where it will go next, so it is with the Spirit. We do not know on whom he will next bestow this life from heaven."

"What do you mean?" Nicodemus asked.

Jesus replied, "You, a respected Jewish teacher, and yet you don't understand these things? I am telling you what I know and have seen—and yet you won't believe me. But if you don't even believe me when I tell you about such things as these that

*Or, "Physical birth is not enough. You must also be born spiritually. . . ." This alternate paraphrase interprets "born of water" as meaning the normal process observed during every human birth. Some think this means water baptism.

21

happen here among men, how can you possibly believe if I tell you what is going on in heaven? For only I, the Messiah, have come to earth and will return to heaven again. And as Moses in the wilderness lifted up the bronze image of a serpent on a pole, even so I must be lifted up upon a pole, so that anyone who believes in me will have eternal life. For God loved the world so much that he gave his only Son so that anyone who believes in him shall not perish but have eternal life. God did not send his Son into the world to condemn it, but to save it.

"There is no eternal doom awaiting those who trust him to save them. But those who don't trust him have already been tried and condemned for not believing in the only Son of God.

"Their sentence is based on this fact: that the Light from heaven came into the world, but they loved the darkness more than the Light, for their deeds were evil. They hated the heavenly Light because they wanted to sin in the darkness. They stayed away from that Light for fear their sins would be exposed and they would be punished. But those doing right come gladly to the Light to let everyone see that they are doing what God wants them to."

John 3: 1–21.

Unforgettable Incident at Jacob's Well

Afterwards Jesus and his disciples left Jerusalem and stayed for a while in Judea.

John the Baptist was not yet in prison. He was baptizing at Aenon, near Salim.

One day someone began an argument with John's disciples, telling them that Jesus' baptism was best. So they came to John and said, "Master, the man you met on the other side of the Jordan River—the one you said was the Messiah—he is baptizing too, and everybody is going over there instead of coming here to us."

John replied, "You yourselves know how plainly I told you that I am not the Messiah. I am here to prepare the way for him —that is all."

When the Lord knew that the Pharisees had heard about the

Unforgettable Incident at Jacob's Well

greater crowds coming to him than to John to be baptized and to become his disciples—(though Jesus himself didn't baptize them, but his disciples did)—he left Judea and returned to the province of Galilee.

He had to go through Samaria on the way, and around noon as he approached the village of Sychar, he came to Jacob's Well located on the parcel of ground Jacob gave to his son Joseph. Jesus was tired from the long walk in the hot sun and sat wearily beside the well.

Soon a Samaritan woman came to draw water, and Jesus asked her for a drink. The woman was surprised that a Jew would ask a "despised Samaritan" for anything—usually they wouldn't even speak to them!—and she remarked about this to Jesus.

He replied, "If you only knew what a wonderful gift God has for you, and who I am, you would ask me for some *living* water!"

"But you don't have a rope or a bucket," she said, "and this is a very deep well! Where would you get this living water? And besides, are you greater than our ancestor Jacob? How can you offer better water than this which he and his sons and cattle enjoyed?"

Jesus replied that people soon became thirsty again after drinking this water. "But the water I give them," he said, "becomes a perpetual spring within them, watering them forever with eternal life."

"Please, sir," the woman said, "give me some of that water! Then I'll never be thirsty again and won't have to make this long trip out here every day."

"Go and get your husband," Jesus told her.

"But I'm not married," the woman replied.

"All too true!" Jesus said. "For you have had five husbands, and you aren't even married to the man you're living with now."

"Sir," the woman said, "you must be a prophet. But say, tell me, why is it that you Jews insist that Jerusalem is the only place of worship, while we Samaritans claim it is here at Mount Gerazim, where our ancestors worshiped?"

Jesus replied, "The time is coming, ma'am, when we will no longer be concerned about whether to worship the Father here or in Jerusalem. For it's not *where* we worship that counts, but *how* we worship—is our worship spiritual and real? Do we have the Holy Spirit's help? For God is Spirit, and we must have his help to worship as we should. The Father wants this kind of worship from us. But you Samaritans know so little about him, worshiping blindly, while we Jews know all about him, for salvation comes to the world through the Jews."

The woman said, "Well, at least I know that the Messiah will come—the one they call Christ—and when he does, he will explain everything to us."

Then Jesus told her, "I am the Messiah!"

The woman left her waterpot beside the well and went back to the village and told everyone, "Come and meet a man who told me everything I ever did! Can this be the Messiah?" So the people came streaming from the village to see him.

Meanwhile, the disciples were urging Jesus to eat. "No," he said, "I have some food you don't know about."

"Who brought it to him?" the disciples asked each other.

Then Jesus explained: "My nourishment comes from doing the will of God who sent me, and from finishing his work. Do you think the work of harvesting will not begin until the summer ends four months from now? Look around you! Vast fields of human souls are ripening all around us, and are ready now for reaping. The reapers will be paid good wages and will be gathering eternal souls into the granaries of heaven! What joys await the sower and the reaper, both together! For it is true that one sows and someone else reaps. I sent you to reap where you didn't sow; others did the work, and you received the harvest."

Many from the Samaritan village believed he was the Messiah because of the woman's report: "He told me everything I ever did!" They begged him to stay at their village; and he did, for two days.

John 3: 22 . . . 28; 4: 1–40.

"Your Son Is Healed!"

At the end of two days' stay Jesus went on into Galilee. He used to say, "A prophet is honored everywhere except in his own country!" But the Galileans welcomed him with open arms, for they had been in Jerusalem at the Passover celebration and had seen some of his miracles.

In the course of his journey through Galilee he arrived at the town of Cana, where he had turned the water into wine. While he was there, a man in the city of Capernaum, a government official whose son was very sick, went over to Cana, found Jesus, and begged him to come to Capernaum with him and heal his son, who was now at death's door.

Jesus asked, "Won't any of you believe in me unless I do more and more miracles?"

The official pled, "Sir, please come now before my child dies."

Then Jesus told him, "Go back home. Your son is healed!" And the man believed Jesus and started home.

While he was on his way, some of his servants met him with the news that all was well—his son had recovered. He asked them when the lad had begun to feel better, and they replied, "Yesterday afternoon at about one o'clock his fever suddenly disappeared!" Then the father realized it was the same moment that Jesus had told him, "Your son is healed."

John 4: 43–53.

Healing at Pool of Bethesda

Afterwards Jesus returned to Jerusalem for one of the Jewish religious holidays. Inside the city was Bethesda Pool, with five covered platforms or porches surrounding it. Crowds of sick folks—lame, blind, or with paralyzed limbs—lay on the platforms (waiting for a certain movement of the water, for an angel of the Lord came from time to time and disturbed the water, and the first person to step down into it afterwards was healed).

One of the men lying there had been sick for thirty-eight years. When Jesus saw him and knew how long he had been ill, he asked him, "Would you like to get well?"

"I can't," the sick man said, "for I have no one to help me into the pool at the movement of the water. While I am trying to get there, someone else always gets in ahead of me."

Jesus told him, "Stand up, roll up your sleeping mat and go on home!" Instantly, the man was healed! He rolled up the mat and began walking!

But it was on the Sabbath when this miracle was done. So the Jewish leaders objected. They said to the man who was cured, "You can't work on the Sabbath! It's illegal to carry that sleeping mat!"

"The man who healed me told me to," was his reply.

"Who said such a thing as that?" they demanded.

The man didn't know, and Jesus had disappeared into the crowd. But afterwards Jesus found him in the Temple and told him, "Now you are well; don't sin as you did before, or something even worse may happen to you."

Then the man went to find the Jewish leaders and told them it was Jesus who had healed him. So they began harassing Jesus as a Sabbath breaker. But Jesus replied, "My Father constantly does good, and I'm following his example."

Then the Jewish leaders were all the more eager to kill him because in addition to disobeying their Sabbath laws, he had spoken of God as his Father, thereby making himself equal with God.

Jesus replied, "The Son can do nothing by himself. He does only what he sees the Father doing, and in the same way. For the Father loves the Son, and tells him everything he is doing; and the Son will do far more awesome miracles than this man's healing. He will even raise from the dead anyone he wants to, just as the Father does. And the Father leaves all judgment of sin to his Son, so that everyone will honor the Son, just as they honor the Father. But if you refuse to honor God's Son, whom he sent to you, then you are certainly not honoring the Father.

"I say emphatically that anyone who listens to my message and believes in God who sent me has eternal life, and will never be damned for his sins, but has already passed out of death into life. And I solemnly declare that the time is coming, in fact, it is here, when the dead shall hear my voice—the voice of the Son of God—and those who listen shall live. The Father has life in himself, and has granted his Son to have life in himself, and to judge the sins of all mankind because he is the Son of Man. Don't be so surprised! Indeed the time is coming when all the dead in their graves shall hear the voice of God's Son, and shall rise again—those who have done good, to eternal life; and those who have continued in evil, to judgment.

"But I pass no judgment without consulting the Father. I judge as I am told. And my judgment is absolutely fair and just, for it is according to the will of God who sent me and is not merely my own.

"When I make claims about myself they aren't believed, but someone else, yes, John the Baptist, is making these claims for me too. You have gone out to listen to his preaching, and I can assure you that all he says about me is true! But the truest witness I have is not from a man, though I have reminded you about John's witness so that you will believe in me and be saved. John shone brightly for a while, and you benefited and rejoiced, but I have a greater witness than John. I refer to the miracles I do; these have been assigned me by the Father, and they prove that the Father has sent me. And the Father himself has also testified about me, though not appearing to you personally, or speaking to you directly. But you are not listening to him, for you refuse to believe me—the one sent to you with God's message.

"You search the Scriptures, for you believe they give you eternal life. And the Scriptures point to me! Yet you won't come to me so that I can give you this life eternal!

"Your approval or disapproval means nothing to me, for as I know so well, you don't have God's love within you. I know,

27

because I have come to you representing my Father and you refuse to welcome me, though you readily enough receive those who aren't sent from him, but represent only themselves! No wonder you can't believe! For you gladly honor each other, but you don't care about the honor that comes from the only God!

"Yet it is not I who will accuse you of this to the Father—Moses will! Moses, on whose laws you set your hopes of heaven. For you have refused to believe Moses. He wrote about me, but you refuse to believe him, so you refuse to believe in me. And since you don't believe what he wrote, no wonder you don't believe me either."

John 5: 1–47.

3 Preacher

Sermon in Home Town

Then Jesus returned to Galilee, full of the Holy Spirit's power. Soon he became well known throughout all that region for his sermons in the synagogues; everyone praised him.

When he came to the village of Nazareth, his boyhood home, he went as usual to the synagogue on Saturday, and stood up to read the Scriptures. He opened it to the place where it says:

"The Spirit of the Lord is upon me; he has appointed me to preach Good News to the poor; he has sent me to heal the brokenhearted and to announce that captives shall be released and the blind shall see, that the downtrodden shall be freed from their oppressors, and that God is ready to give blessings to all who come to him."

He closed the book and handed it back to the attendant and sat down, while everyone in the synagogue gazed at him intently. Then he added, "These scriptures came true today!"

All who were there spoke well of him and were amazed by the beautiful words that fell from his lips. "How can this be?" they asked. "Isn't this Joseph's son?"

Then Jesus said, "Probably you will quote me that proverb, 'Physician, heal yourself'—meaning, 'Why don't you do miracles here in your home town like those you did in Capernaum?'

"But I solemnly declare to you that no prophet is accepted in his own home town! For example, remember how Elijah the prophet used a miracle to help the widow of Zarephath—a foreigner from the land of Sidon. There were many Jewish widows needing help in those days of famine, for there had been no rain for three and one-half years, and hunger stalked the land; yet Elijah was not sent to them.

"Or think of the prophet Elisha, who healed Naaman, a Syrian, rather than the many Jewish lepers needing help."

These remarks stung them to fury; and jumping up, they mobbed him and took him to the edge of the hill on which the city was built, to push him over the cliff. But he walked away through the crowd and left them.

When Jesus heard that John had been arrested, he left Judea and returned home to Nazareth in Galilee; but soon he moved to Capernaum, beside the Lake of Galilee, and preached God's Good News there in the synagogue every Saturday.

"At last the time has come!" he announced. "God's Kingdom is near! Turn from your sins and act on this glorious news! Turn from sin, and turn to God, for the Kingdom of heaven is near."

Luke 4: 14–31; Mark 1: 15; Matthew 4: 12, 13, 17.

Choosing Disciples and Preaching

One day as Jesus was walking along the shores of the Sea of Galilee, he saw Simon and his brother Andrew fishing with nets, for they were commercial fishermen.

Jesus called out to them, "Come, follow me! And I will make you fishermen for the souls of men!" At once they left their nets and went along with him.

A little further up the beach he saw two other brothers, James and John, sitting in a boat with their father, Zebedee, mending their nets, and he called to them to come too. At once they stopped their work and left their father behind with the hired servants and went with him.

Jesus and his companions now arrived at the town of Capernaum and on Saturday morning went into the Jewish place of worship—the synagogue—where he preached. The congregation was surprised at his sermon because he spoke as an authority, and didn't try to prove his points by quoting others—quite unlike what they were used to hearing!

A man possessed by a demon was present and began shouting. "Why are you bothering us, Jesus of Nazareth—have you come to destroy us demons? I know who you are—the holy Son of God!"

Jesus curtly commanded the demon to say no more and to come out of the man. At that the evil spirit screamed and convulsed the man violently and then left him without hurting him further.

Then, leaving the synagogue, Jesus and his disciples went over to Simon and Andrew's home.

The next morning Jesus was up long before daybreak and went out alone into the wilderness to pray. The crowds searched everywhere for him and when they finally found him they begged him not to leave them, but to stay at Capernaum. But he replied, "I must preach the Good News of the Kingdom of God in other places too, for that is why I was sent."

Later, Simon and the others went out to find him, and told him, "Everyone is asking for you."

But he replied, "We must go on to other towns as well, and give my message to them too, for that is why I came."

Jesus traveled all through Galilee teaching in the Jewish synagogues, everywhere preaching the Good News about the Kingdom of Heaven. The report of his miracles spread as far away as Syria. Enormous crowds followed him wherever he went—people from Galilee, and the Ten Cities, and Jerusalem, and from all over Judea, and even from across the Jordan River.

Mark 1: 16–26; 29: 35–38; Luke 4: 32, 35, 42–43; Matthew 4: 21–25.

Greatest Sermon of All Time

One day as the crowds were gathering, Jesus went up the hillside with his disciples and sat down and taught them there.

"Humble men are very fortunate!" he told them, "for the Kingdom of Heaven is given to them.

"Those who mourn are fortunate! for they shall be comforted.

"The meek and lowly are fortunate! for the whole wide world belongs to them.

"Happy are those who long to be just and good, for they shall be completely satisfied.

"Happy are the kind and merciful, for they shall be shown mercy.

"Happy are those whose hearts are pure, for they shall see God.

"Happy are those who strive for peace—they shall be called the sons of God.

"Happy are those who are persecuted because they are good, for the Kingdom of Heaven is theirs.

"When you are reviled and persecuted and lied about because you are my followers—wonderful! Be *happy* about it! Be *very glad!* for a *tremendous reward* awaits you up in heaven. And remember, the ancient prophets were persecuted, too.

"You are the world's seasoning, to make it tolerable. If you lose your flavor, what will happen to the world? And you yourselves will be thrown out and trampled underfoot as worthless.

"You are the world's light—a city on a hill, glowing in the night for all to see. Don't hide your light! Let it shine for all; let your good deeds glow for all to see, so that they will praise your heavenly Father.

"Don't misunderstand why I have come—it isn't to cancel the laws of Moses and the warnings of the prophets. No, I came to fulfill them, and to make them all come true. With all the earnestness I have I say: Every law in the Book will continue until its purpose is achieved.

"And so if anyone breaks the least commandment, and teaches others to, he shall be the least in the Kingdom of Heaven. But those who teach God's laws *and obey them* shall be great in the Kingdom of Heaven.

"But I warn you—unless your goodness is greater than that of the Pharisees and other Jewish leaders, you can't get into the Kingdom of Heaven at all!

"Under the laws of Moses the rule was, 'If you kill, you must die.' But I have added to that rule, and tell you that if you are only *angry*, even in your own home, you are in danger of judgment! If you call your friend an idiot, you are in danger of being brought before the court. And if you curse him, you are in danger of the fires of hell.

"So if you are standing before the altar in the Temple, offering a sacrifice to God, and suddenly remember that a friend has something against you, leave your sacrifice there beside the altar and go and apologize and be reconciled to him, and then come and offer your sacrifice to God.

"Come to terms quickly with your enemy before it is too late and he drags you into court and you are thrown into a debtor's cell, for you will stay there until you have paid the last penny.

"The laws of Moses said, 'You shall not commit adultery.' But I say: Anyone who even looks at a woman with lust in his eye has already committed adultery with her in his heart.

"So if your eye—even if it is your best eye! —causes you to lust, gouge it out and throw it away. Better for part of you to be destroyed than for all of you to be cast into hell.

"And if your hand—even your right hand—causes you to sin, cut it off and throw it away. Better that than find yourself in hell.

"The law of Moses says, 'If anyone wants to be rid of his wife, he can divorce her merely by giving her a letter of dismissal.' But I say that a man who divorces his wife, except for fornication, causes her to commit adultery if she marries again. And he who marries her commits adultery.

"Again, the law of Moses says, 'You shall not break your vows to God, but must fulfill them all.' But I say: don't make any vows! And even to say, 'By heavens!' is a sacred vow to God, for the heavens are God's throne. And if you say 'By the earth!' it is a sacred vow, for the earth is his footstool. And don't swear 'By Jerusalem!' for Jerusalem is the capital of the great King. Don't even swear 'By my head!' for you can't turn one hair white or black. Say just a simple 'Yes, I will' or 'No, I won't.' Your word is enough. To strengthen your promise with a vow shows that something is wrong.

"The law of Moses says, 'If a man gouges out another's eye, he must pay with his own eye. If a tooth gets knocked out, knock out the tooth of the one who did it.' But I say: Don't resist violence! If you are slapped on one cheek, turn the other too. If you are ordered to court, and your shirt is taken from you, give your coat too. If the military demand that you carry their gear for a mile, carry it two. Give to those who ask, and don't turn away from those who want to borrow.

"There is a saying, 'Love your *friends* and hate your enemies.' But I say: Love your *enemies!* Pray for those who *persecute* you! In that way you will be acting as true sons of your Father in heaven. For he gives his sunlight to both the evil and the good, and sends rain on the just and on the unjust too.

"If you love only those who love you, what good is that? Even scoundrels do that much. If you are friendly only to your friends, how are you different from anyone else? Even the heathen do that.

"But you are to be perfect, even as your Father in heaven is perfect."

Matthew 5: 1–48.

Noblest of All Prayers

"Take care! Don't do your good deeds publicly, to be admired, for then you will lose the reward from your Father in heaven. When you give a gift to a beggar, don't shout about it as the hypocrites do—blowing trumpets in the synagogues and streets to call attention to their acts of charity! I tell you in all earnestness, they have received all the reward they will ever get. But when you do a kindness to someone, do it secretly— don't tell your left hand what your right hand is doing. And your Father who knows all secrets will reward you.

"And now about prayer. When you pray, don't be like the hypocrites who pretend piety by praying publicly on street corners and in the synagogues where everyone can see them. Truly, that is all the reward they will ever get. But when you pray, go away by yourself, all alone, and shut the door behind

34

you and pray to your Father secretly, and your Father, who knows your secrets, will reward you.

"Don't recite the same prayer over and over as the heathen do, who think prayers are answered only by repeating them again and again. Remember, your Father knows exactly what you need even before you ask him!

"Pray along these lines:

" 'Our Father in heaven, we honor your holy name. We ask that your kingdom will come now. May your will be done here on earth, just as it is in heaven.

" 'Give us our food again today, as usual, and forgive us our sins, just as we have forgiven those who have sinned against us.

" 'Don't bring us into temptation, but deliver us from the Evil One.* Amen.'

"Your heavenly Father will forgive you if you forgive those who sin against you; but if *you* refuse to forgive *them,* he will not forgive *you.*

"And now about fasting. When you fast, declining your food for a spiritual purpose, don't do it publicly, as the hypocrites do, who try to look wan and disheveled so people will feel sorry for them. Truly, that is the only reward they will ever get. But when you fast, put on festive clothing, so that no one will suspect you are hungry, except your Father who knows every secret. And he will reward you.

"Don't store up treasures here on earth where they can erode away or may be stolen. Store them in heaven where they will never lose their value, and are safe from thieves. If your profits are in heaven your heart will be there too.

"If your eye is pure, there will be sunshine in your soul. But if your eye is clouded with evil thoughts and desires, you are in deep spiritual darkness. And oh, how deep that darkness can be!

"You cannot serve two masters; God and money. For you will

*Or, "from evil." Some manuscripts add here, "For yours is the kingdom and the power and the glory forever. Amen."

hate one and love the other, or else the other way around.

"So my counsel is: Don't worry about *things*—food, drink, and clothes. For you already have life and a body—and they are far more important than what to eat and wear. Look at the birds! They don't worry about what to eat—they don't need to sow or reap or store up food—for your heavenly Father feeds them. And you are far more valuable to him than they are. Will all your worries add a single moment to your life?

"And why worry about your clothes? Look at the field lilies! They don't worry about theirs. Yet King Solomon in all his glory was not clothed as beautifully as they. And if God cares so wonderfully for flowers that are here today and gone tomorrow, won't he more surely care for you, O men of little faith?

"So don't worry at all about having enough food and clothing. Why be like the heathen? For they take pride in all these things and are deeply concerned about them. But your heavenly Father already knows perfectly well that you need them.

"And he will give them to you if you give him first place in your life and live as he wants you to. So don't be anxious about tomorrow. God will take care of your tomorrow too. Live one day at a time."

Matthew 6: 1–34.

The House on the Rock

"Don't criticize, and then you won't be criticized. For others will treat you as you treat them.

"Why worry about a speck in the eye of a brother when you have a board in your own? Should you say, 'Friend, let me help you get that speck out of your eye,' when you can't even see because of the board in your own? Hypocrite! First get rid of the board. Then you can see to help your brother.

"Don't give holy things to depraved men. Don't give pearls to swine! They will trample the pearls and turn and attack you.

"Ask, and you will be given what you ask for. Seek, and you will find. Knock, and the door will be opened. For everyone who asks, receives. Anyone who seeks, finds. If only you will knock, the door will open.

The House on the Rock

"If a child asks his father for a loaf of bread, will he be given a stone instead? If he asks for fish, will he be given a poisonous snake? Of course not! And if you hardhearted, sinful men know how to give good gifts to your children, won't your Father in heaven even more certainly give good gifts to those who ask him for them?

"Do for others what you want them to do for you. This is the teaching of the laws of Moses in a nutshell.

"Heaven can be entered only through the narrow gate! The highway to hell is broad, and its gate is wide enough for all the multitudes who choose its easy way. But the Gateway to Life is small, and the road is narrow, and only a few ever find it.

"Beware of false teachers who come disguised as harmless sheep, but are wolves and will tear you apart. You can detect them by the way they act, just as you can identify a tree by its fruit. You need never confuse grapevines with thorn bushes or figs with thistles. Different kinds of fruit trees can quickly be identified by examining their fruit. A variety that produces delicious fruit never produces an inedible kind. And a tree producing an inedible kind can't produce what is good. So the trees having the inedible fruit are chopped down and thrown on the fire. Yes, the way to identify a tree or a person is by the kind of fruit produced.

"Not all who sound religious are really godly people. They may refer to me as 'Lord,' but still won't get to heaven. For the decisive question is whether they obey my Father in heaven. At the Judgment many will tell me, 'Lord, Lord, we told others about you and used your name to cast out demons and to do many other great miracles.' But I will reply, 'You have never been mine. Go away, for your deeds are evil.'

"All who listen to my instructions and follow them are wise, like a man who builds his house on solid rock. Though the rain comes in torrents, and the floods rise and the storm winds beat against his house, it won't collapse, for it is built on rock.

"But those who hear my instructions and ignore them are foolish, like a man who builds his house on sand. For when the rains and floods come, and storm winds beat against his house, it will fall with a mighty crash."

The crowds were amazed at Jesus' sermons, for he taught as one who had great authority, and not as their Jewish leaders.

Matthew 7: 1–29.

4 Popularity

Fishers of Men

Large crowds followed Jesus as he came down the hillside.

Look! A leper is approaching. He kneels before him, worshiping. "Sir," the leper pleads, "if you want to, you can heal me!" Jesus touches the man. "I want to! Be healed!"

And instantly the leprosy disappears. Then Jesus says to him, "Don't stop to talk to anyone; go right over to the priest to be examined, and take with you the offering required by Moses' law for lepers who are healed—a public testimony of your cure."

But as the man went on his way he began to shout the good news that he was healed; as a result, such throngs soon surrounded Jesus that he couldn't publicly enter a city anywhere, but had to stay out in the barren wastelands. And people from everywhere came to him there.

One day as he was preaching on the shore of Lake Gennesaret, great crowds pressed in on him to listen to the Word of God. He noticed two empty boats standing at the water's edge while the fishermen washed their nets. Stepping into one of the boats, Jesus asked Simon, its owner, to push out a little into the water, so that he could sit in the boat and speak to the crowds from there.

When he had finished speaking, he said to Simon, "Now go out where it is deeper and let down your nets and you will catch a lot of fish!"

"Sir," Simon replied, "we worked hard all last night and didn't catch a thing. But if you say so, we'll try again."

And this time their nets were so full that they began to tear!

A shout for help brought their partners in the other boat and soon both boats were filled with fish and on the verge of sinking.

When Simon Peter realized what had happened, he fell to his knees before Jesus and said, "Oh, sir, please leave us—I'm too much of a sinner for you to have around." For he was awestruck by the size of their catch, and his partners too—James and John.

Jesus replied, "Don't be afraid! From now on you'll be fishing for the souls of men!" And as soon as they landed, they left everything and went with Jesus.

Several days later he returned to Capernaum, and the news of his arrival spread quickly through the city. Soon the house where he was staying was so packed with visitors that there wasn't room for a single person more, not even outside the door. And he preached the Word to them.

Four men arrived carrying a paralyzed man. They couldn't get to Jesus through the crowd. So they went up on the roof above him, took off some tiles and lowered the sick man down into the crowd, still on his sleeping mat, right in front of Jesus.

When Jesus saw their faith, he said to the sick man, "Cheer up, son! For I have forgiven your sins!"

But some of the Jewish religious leaders said to themselves as they sat there, "What? This is blasphemy! Does he think he is God? For only God can forgive sins."

Jesus knew what they were thinking and asked them, "Why are you thinking such evil thoughts? I, the Messiah, have the authority on earth to forgive sins. But talk is cheap—anybody could say that. So I'll prove it to you by healing this man." Then, turning to the paralyzed man, he commanded, "Pick up your stretcher and go on home, for you are healed."

Immediately, the man jumped to his feet, picked up his mat and went home.

Matthew 8: 1–4; 9: 2–6; Mark 1: 41–45; 2: 1–7; Luke 5: 1–12, 15, 19, 25.

Calls Matthew

Jesus went out to the seashore again and preached to the crowds.

As Jesus was going on down the road, he saw a tax collector, Matthew* (the man's name was Levi), sitting at a tax collection booth. Jesus said to him, "Come be my disciple."

And Levi jumped to his feet and went along.

Levi held a reception in his home with Jesus as the guest of honor. Many of Levi's fellow tax collectors and many notorious swindlers were there as guests!

But the Pharisees and teachers of the Law complained bitterly to Jesus' disciples about his eating with such notorious sinners. They said to his disciples, "Why does your teacher associate with men like that?"

When Jesus heard what they were saying, he told them, "People who are well don't need a doctor! It's the sick people who do! Now go away and learn the meaning of this verse of Scripture, 'It isn't your sacrifices and your gifts I want—I want you to be merciful.' For I have come to urge sinners, not the self-righteous, back to God."

The disciples of John the Baptist came to Jesus and said, "John's disciples sometimes fast. Why don't your disciples fast?"

Jesus replied, "Do friends of the bridegroom refuse to eat at the wedding feast? Should they be sad while he is with them? But some day he will be taken away from them, and then they will mourn."

Then Jesus used these illustrations: "It is like patching an old garment with unshrunk cloth! What happens? The patch pulls away and leaves the hole worse than before, and the old garment will look worse with a new patch on it!

"And who would use old wineskins to store new wine? For the old skins would burst with the pressure, and the wine would be spilled and the skins ruined. But no one after drinking

*The Matthew who wrote this book.

the old wine seems to want the fresh and the new. 'The old ways are best,' they say."

Luke 5: 27–30; 36–39; Matthew 9: 9–17; Mark 2: 13–21.

His Enemies Conspire

One Sabbath as Jesus and his disciples were walking through some grainfields, they were breaking off the heads of wheat, rubbing off the husks in their hands and eating the grains. Some Pharisees saw them do it and protested, "Your disciples are breaking the law. They are harvesting on the Sabbath."

Jesus replied, "Don't you read the Scriptures? Haven't you ever read what King David did when he and his men were hungry? He went into the house of God—Abiathar was High Priest then—and they ate the special bread only priests were allowed to eat. That was against the law too.

"And haven't you ever read in the law of Moses how the priests on duty in the Temple may work on the Sabbath? And truly, one is here who is greater than the Temple! But if you had known the meaning of this Scripture verse, 'I want you to be merciful more than I want your offerings,' you would not have condemned those who aren't guilty!

"The Sabbath was made to benefit man, and not man to benefit the Sabbath. And I, the Messiah, have authority even to decide what men can do on Sabbath days!"

On another Sabbath Jesus was in the synagogue teaching. A man was present whose right hand was deformed. The teachers of the Law and the Pharisees watched closely to see whether he would heal the man that day, since it was the Sabbath. How well he knew their thoughts! But he said to the man, "Come and stand here where everyone can see." So he did.

Then Jesus said, "I have a question for you. Is it right to do good on the Sabbath day, or to do harm? To save life, or to destroy it?" But they wouldn't answer him.

This was Jesus' answer: "If you had just one sheep, and it fell into a well on the Sabbath, would you work to rescue it that day? Of course you would. And how much more valuable is a person than a sheep! Yes, it is right to do good on the Sabbath."

Looking around at them angrily, for he was deeply disturbed by their indifference to human need, he said to the man, "Reach out your hand." And as he did, it became completely normal again.

At once the Pharisees went away and met with the Herodians to discuss plans for killing Jesus. He knew what they were planning, and left the synagogue and with his disciples withdrew to the beach, but he cautioned them against spreading the news about his miracles.

Afterwards Jesus went up into the hills and called together his followers and chose twelve of them to be the inner circle of his disciples. (They were appointed as his "apostles," or "missionaries") to go out to preach and to cast out demons.

The Jewish teachers of religion said, "His trouble is that he's possessed by Satan, king of demons. That's why demons obey him."

Jesus summoned these men and asked them (using proverbs they all understood), "How can Satan cast out Satan? A kingdom divided against itself will collapse. A home filled with strife and division destroys itself. And if Satan is fighting against himself, how can he accomplish anything? He would never survive.

"Satan must be bound before his demons are cast out, just as a strong man must be tied up before his house can be ransacked and his property robbed.

"I solemnly declare that any sin of man can be forgiven, even blasphemy against me; but blasphemy against the Holy Spirit can never be forgiven. It is an eternal sin."

He told them this because they were saying he did his miracles by Satan's power instead of acknowledging it was by the Holy Spirit's power.

"When a demon is cast out of a man, it goes to the deserts, searching there for rest; but finding none, it returns to the person it left, and finds that its former home is all swept and clean. Then it goes and gets seven other demons more evil than

43

itself, and they all enter the man. And so the poor fellow is seven times worse off then he was before."

Matthew 12: 2–16; Mark 2: 26–28; 3: 4–7; 13; 22–30; Luke 6: 1–13; 11: 24–26.

Great Sermon on the Plain

Jesus went out into the mountains and prayed all night. At daybreak he called together his twelve disciples.

Here are the names of his twelve disciples: Simon (also called Peter), Andrew (Peter's brother), James (Zebedee's son), John (James' brother), Philip, Bartholomew, Thomas, Matthew (the tax collector), James (Alphaeus' son), Thaddaeus, Simon (a member of "The Zealots," a subversive political party), Judas Iscariot (the one who betrayed him).

When they came down the slopes of the mountain, they stood with Jesus on a large, level area, surrounded by many of his followers who, in turn, were surrounded by the crowds. For people from all over Judea and from Jerusalem and from as far north as the seacoasts of Tyre and Sidon had come to hear him or to be healed.

Then he turned to his disciples and said,

"What happiness there is for you who are poor, for the Kingdom of God is yours!

"What happiness there is for you who are now hungry, for you are going to be satisfied!

"What happiness there is for you who weep, for the time will come when you shall laugh with joy!

"What happiness it is when others hate you and exclude you and insult you and smear your name because you are mine!

"When that happens, rejoice! Yes, leap for joy! For you will have a great reward awaiting you in heaven. And you will be in good company—the ancient prophets were treated that way too!

"But, oh, the sorrows that await the rich. For they have their only happiness down here. They are fat and prosperous now, but a time of awful hunger is before them. Their careless laughter now means sorrow then.

44

Great Sermon on the Plain

"And what sadness is ahead for those praised by the crowds —for *false* prophets have *always* been praised.

"Listen, all of you.

"Love your *enemies.* Do *good* to those who *hate* you. Pray for the happiness of those who *curse* you; implore God's blessing on those who *hurt* you.

"If someone slaps you on one cheek, let him slap the other too! If someone demands your coat, give him your shirt besides.

"Give what you have to anyone who asks you for it; and when things are taken away from you, don't worry about getting them back.

"Treat others as you want them to treat you.

"Do you think you deserve credit for merely loving those who love you? Even the godless do that! And if you do good only to those who do you good—is that so wonderful? Even sinners do that much! And if you lend money only to those who can repay you, what good is that? Even the most wicked will lend to their own kind for full return!

"Love your *enemies!* Do good to *them!* Lend to *them!* And don't be concerned about the fact that they won't repay. Then your reward from heaven will be very great, and you will truly be acting as sons of God: for he is kind to the *unthankful* and to those who are *very wicked.* Try to show as much compassion as your Father does.

"Never criticize or condemn—or it will all come back on you. Go easy on others; then they will do the same for you.

"For if you give, you will get! Your gift will return to you in full and overflowing measure, pressed down, shaken together to make room for more, and running over. Whatever measure you use to give—large or small—will be used to measure what is given back to you."

Matthew 10: 2–4; Luke 6: 12–38.

45

5 Wisdom

Stories Jesus Used

Here are some of the story-illustrations Jesus used in his sermons: "What good is it for one blind man to lead another? He will fall into a ditch and pull the other down with him. How can a student know more than his teacher? But if he works hard, he may learn as much.

"And why quibble about the speck in someone else's eye —his little fault—when a board is in your own? How can you think of saying to him, 'Brother, let me help you get rid of that speck in your eye,' when you can't see past the board in yours? Hypocrite! First get rid of the board, and then perhaps you can see well enough to deal with his speck!

"A tree from good stock doesn't produce scrub fruit nor do trees from poor stock produce choice fruit. A tree is identified by the kind of fruit it produces. Figs never grow on thorns, or grapes on bramble bushes. A good man produces good deeds from a good heart. And an evil man produces evil deeds from his hidden wickedness. Whatever is in the heart overflows into speech.

"So why do you call me 'Lord' when you won't obey me? But all those who come and listen and obey me are like a man who builds a house on a strong foundation laid upon the underlying rock. When the floodwaters rise and break against the house, it stands firm, for it is strongly built. But those who listen and don't obey are like a man who builds a house without a foundation. When the floods sweep down against that house, it crumbles into a heap of ruins."

Luke 6: 39–49.

Healings in Capernaum and Nain

When Jesus arrived in Capernaum, a Roman army captain came and pled with him to come to his home and heal his servant boy who was in bed paralyzed and racked with pain. Some respected Jewish elders asked him to come and help the man. They told him what a wonderful person the captain was, "for he loves the Jews and even paid personally to build us a synagogue!"

Jesus said, "Yes, I will come and heal him."

Then the officer said, "Sir, I am not worthy to have you in my home; and it isn't necessary for you to come. If you will only stand here and say, 'Be healed,' my servant will get well.

Jesus stood there amazed! Turning to the crowd he said, "I haven't seen faith like this in all the land of Israel! And I tell you this, that many Gentiles, like this Roman officer, shall come from all over the world and sit down in the Kingdom of Heaven with Abraham, Isaac, and Jacob. And many an Israelite—those for whom the Kingdom was prepared—shall be cast into outer darkness, into the place of weeping and torment."

Then Jesus said to the Roman officer, "Go on home. What you have believed has happened!" The boy was healed that same hour!

Not long afterwards, Jesus went with his disciples to the village of Nain, with the usual great crowd at his heels. A funeral procession was coming out as he approached the village gate. The boy who had died was the only son of his widowed mother, and many mourners from the village were with her. When the Lord saw her, his heart overflowed with sympathy. He said, "Don't cry!" Then he walked over to the coffin and touched it, and the bearers stopped. He said, "Laddie, come back to life again." Then the boy sat up and began to talk to those around him!

A great fear swept the crowd, and they exclaimed with praises to God, "A mighty prophet has risen among us."

The report of what he did that day raced from end to end of Judea and even out across the borders. The disciples of John the Baptist heard of all that Jesus was doing and told John about it.

Matthew 8: 5–13; Luke 7: 3–5; 11–18.

Messengers Come from John

Jesus was curing many sick people of their various diseases —healing the lame and the blind and casting out evil spirits. John the Baptist, who was now in prison, heard about the miracles the Messiah was doing, so he sent his disciples to ask Jesus, "Are you really the one we are waiting for, or shall we keep on looking?"

When they asked Jesus John's question, Jesus told them: "Go back to John and tell him all you have seen and heard here today: the blind people I've healed, and the lame people now walking without help, and the cured lepers, and the deaf who hear, and the dead raised to life; and tell him about my preaching the Good News to the poor. Then give him this message, 'Blessed are those who don't doubt me.' "

When John's disciples had gone, Jesus began talking about him to the crowds. "When you went out into the barren wilderness to see John, what did you expect him to be like? Grass blowing in the wind? Or were you expecting to see a man dressed as a prince in a palace? Or a prophet of God? Yes, and he is more than just a prophet. For John is the man mentioned in the Scriptures—a messenger to precede me, to announce my coming, and prepare people to receive me. Truly, of all men ever born, none shines more brightly than John the Baptist. And yet, even the lesser lights in the Kingdom of Heaven will be greater than he is! And from the time John the Baptist began preaching and baptizing until now, ardent multitudes have been crowding toward the Kingdom of Heaven, for all the laws and prophets looked forward to the Messiah. Then John appeared, and if you are willing to understand what I mean, he is Elijah, the one the prophets said would come at the time the Kingdom begins. If ever you were willing to listen, listen now!"

And all who heard John preach—even the most wicked of them—agreed that God's requirements were right, and they were baptized by him. All, that is, except the Pharisees and teachers of Moses' Law. They rejected God's plan for them and refused John's baptism.

Jesus asked, "What shall I say about this nation? These people are like children playing, who say to their little friends, 'We played wedding and you weren't happy, so we played funeral but you weren't sad.' For John the Baptist doesn't even drink wine and often goes without food, and you say, 'He's crazy.' And I, the Messiah, feast and drink, and you complain that I am 'a glutton and a drinking man, and hang around with the worst sort of sinners!' But brilliant men like you can justify your every inconsistency!"

Then he began to pour out his denunciations against the cities where he had done most of his miracles, because they hadn't turned to God. "Woe to you, Chorazin, and woe to you, Bethsaida! For if the miracles I did in your streets had been done in wicked Tyre and Sidon their people would have repented long ago in shame and humility. Truly, Tyre and Sidon will be better off on the Judgment Day than you! And Capernaum, though highly honored, shall go down to hell! For if the marvelous miracles I did in you had been done in Sodom, it would still be here today. Truly, Sodom will be better off at the Judgment Day than you."

And Jesus prayed this prayer: "O Father, Lord of heaven and earth, thank you for hiding the truth from those who think themselves so wise, and for revealing it to little children. Yes, Father, for it pleased you to do it this way! . . .

"Everything has been entrusted to me by my Father. Only the Father knows the Son, and the Father is known only by the Son and by those to whom the Son reveals him. Come to me and I will give you rest—all of you who work so hard beneath a heavy yoke. Wear my yoke—for it fits perfectly—and let me teach you; for I am gentle and humble, and you shall find rest for your souls; for I give you only light burdens."

Matthew 11: 2–15; 16–30; Luke 7: 24–35.

Story of the Perfume Flask

One of the Pharisees asked Jesus to come to his home for lunch and Jesus accepted the invitation. As they sat down to eat, a woman of the streets—a prostitute—heard he was there and brought an exquisite flask filled with expensive perfume. Going in, she knelt at his feet, weeping, and she wiped them off with her hair and kissed them and poured the perfume on them.

When Jesus' host, a Pharisee, saw what was happening and who the woman was, he said to himself, "This proves that Jesus is no prophet, for if God had really sent him, he would know what kind of woman this one is!"

Then Jesus spoke up and answered his thoughts. "Simon," he said to the Pharisee, "I have something to say to you.

"A man loaned money to two people—$5,000 to one and $500 to the other. But neither of them could pay him back, so he kindly forgave them both, letting them keep the money! Which do you suppose loved him most after that?"

"I suppose the one who had owed him the most." Simon answered.

"Correct," Jesus agreed.

Then he turned to the woman and said to Simon, "Look! See this woman kneeling here! When I entered your home, you didn't bother to offer me water to wash the dust from my feet, but she has washed them with her tears and wiped them with her hair. You refused me the customary kiss of greeting, but she has kissed my feet again and again from the time I first came in. You neglected the usual courtesy of olive oil to anoint my head, but she has covered my feet with rare perfume. Therefore her sins—and they are many—are forgiven, for she loved me much; but one who is forgiven little, shows little love."

And he said to her, "Your sins are forgiven."

Story of the Perfume Flask

Then the men at the table said to themselves, "Who does this man think he is, going around forgiving sins?"

And Jesus said to the woman, "Your faith has saved you; go in peace."

Luke 7: 36–50.

Then a demon-possessed man—he was both blind and unable to talk—was brought to Jesus, and Jesus healed him so that he could both speak and see.

The crowd was amazed. "Maybe Jesus is the Messiah!" they exclaimed.

But the Pharisees said, "He can cast out demons because he is Satan, king of devils."

Jesus knew their thoughts and replied, "A divided kingdom ends in ruin. A city or home divided against itself cannot stand. And if Satan is casting out Satan, he is fighting himself, and destroying his own kingdom. How can his kingdom survive? And if I am empowered by Satan, what about your own followers? For they cast out demons! Do you think this proves they are possessed by Satan? Ask *them* if you are right! But if I am casting out demons because of power from God, it proves that the Kingdom of God has arrived.

"One cannot rob Satan's kingdom without first binding Satan. Only then can his demons be cast out! For when Satan, strong and fully armed, guards his palace, it is safe—until someone stronger and better-armed attacks and overcomes him and strips him of his weapons and carries off his belongings.

"Anyone who isn't helping me is harming me. Even blasphemy against me or any other sin can be forgiven—all except one: speaking against the Holy Spirit shall never be forgiven, either in this world or in the world to come.

"A tree is identified by its fruit. A tree from a select variety produces good fruit; poor varieties don't.

"You brood of snakes! How could evil men like you speak what is good and right? For a man's heart determines his speech. A good man's speech reveals the rich treasures within him. An evil-hearted man is filled with venom, and his speech reveals it. And I tell you this, that you must give account on Judgment Day for every idle word you speak. Your words now reflect your fate then: either you will be justified by them or you will be condemned."

Matthew 12: 22–37; Luke 11: 18–22; Mark 3: 22–29.

One day some of the Jewish leaders, including some Pharisees, came to Jesus asking him to show them a miracle. But Jesus replied, "Only an evil, faithless nation would ask for further proof; and none will be given except what happened to Jonah the prophet! For as Jonah was in the great fish for three days and three nights, so I, the Messiah, shall be in the heart of the earth three days and three nights. The men of Nineveh shall arise against this nation at the judgment and condemn you. For when Jonah preached to them, they repented and turned to God from all their evil ways. And now a greater than Jonah is here —and you refuse to believe him. The Queen of Sheba shall rise against this nation in the judgment, and condemn it; for she came from a distant land to hear the wisdom of Solomon; and now a greater than Solomon is here—and you refuse to believe him.

"This evil nation is like a man possessed by a demon. For if the demon leaves, it goes into the deserts for a while, seeking rest but finding none. Then it says, 'I will return to the man I came from.' So it returns and finds the man's heart clean but empty! Then the demon finds seven other spirits more evil than itself, and all enter the man and live in him. And so he is worse off than before."

Matthew 12: 38–45.

Parable of the Seeds

As Jesus was speaking in a crowded house his mother and brothers were outside wanting to talk with him. They couldn't get into the house because of the crowds. When someone told him they were there, he remarked, "Who is my mother? Who are my brothers?"

Parable of the Seeds

Looking at those around him, he pointed. "Look!" he said, "these are my mother and brothers." Then he added, "Anyone who obeys my Father in heaven is my brother, sister and mother! My mother and my brothers are all those who hear the message of God and obey it."

Later that same day, Jesus left the house and went down to the shore, where a large crowd was gathering to hear him—while many others were still on the way, coming from other towns. So he got into a boat and sat down and talked from there while the people listened on the beach. His usual method of teaching was to tell the people stories, such as this one:

"Listen! A farmer decided to sow some grain. As he scattered the seed on the ground, some of it fell on a footpath and was trampled on, and the birds came and picked it off the hard ground and ate it.

"And some fell on rocky soil where there was little depth of earth; the plants sprang up quickly enough in the shallow soil, but the hot sun soon scorched them and they withered and died, for they had so little root.

"Other seeds fell among thorns that shot up and crowded the young plants so that they produced no grain.

"But some fell on good soil, and produced a crop that was thirty, sixty, and even a hundred times as much as he had planted. If you have ears, listen!"

Afterwards, when he was alone, his disciples came and asked him, "Why do you always use these hard-to-understand illustrations?"

He replied, "God has granted you to know the meaning of these parables for they tell a great deal about the Kingdom of God. But these crowds hear the words and do not understand. For to him who has will more be given," he told them, "and he will have great plenty; but from him who has not, even the little he has will be taken away. That is why I use these illustrations, so people will hear and see but not understand.

"This fulfills the prophecy of Isaiah: 'They hear, but don't understand; they look, but don't see! For their hearts are fat and heavy, and their ears are dull, and they have closed their eyes in sleep, so they won't see and hear and understand and turn to God again, and let me heal them.'

"But blessed are your eyes, for they see; and your ears, for they hear. Many a prophet and godly man has longed to see what you have seen, and hear what you have heard, but couldn't. But if you can't understand *this* simple illustration, what will you do about all the others I am going to tell?

"This is the meaning of the story I told about the farmer planting grain: The seed is God's message to men. The farmer is anyone who brings God's message to others, trying to plant good seed within their lives. The hard path where some of the seeds fell represents the heart of a person who hears the Good News about the Kingdom and doesn't understand it; then Satan comes and snatches away the seeds from his heart and prevents people from believing and being saved.

"The shallow, rocky soil represents the heart of a man who hears the message and receives it with real joy, but somehow the message never really gets through and doesn't take root and grow. He knows the message is true, and sort of believes for awhile; but after a while when trouble comes, or persecution begins because of his beliefs, his enthusiasm fades, and he drops out.

"The thorny ground represents the hearts of people who listen to the Good News and receive it but whose faith afterwards is choked out by worry and riches and the responsibilities and pleasures of life. The delights of wealth, and the search for success and lure of nice things come in and crowd out God's message from their hearts, and so they are never able to help anyone else to believe the Good News.

"But the good soil represents the hearts of those who listen to God's words and cling to them; who truly accept God's message and go out and bring thirty, sixty, or even a hundred others into the Kingdom.

Here is another illustration Jesus used: "The Kingdom of

Let Your Light Shine

Heaven is like a farmer sowing good seed in his field; but one night as he slept, his enemy came and sowed thistles among the wheat. When the crop began to grow, the thistles grew too. The farmer's men came and told him, 'Sir, the field where you planted that choice seed is full of thistles!' 'An enemy has done it,' he exclaimed. 'Shall we pull out the thistles?' they asked. 'No,' he replied. 'You'll hurt the wheat if you do. Let both grow together until the harvest, and I will tell the reapers to sort out the thistles and burn them, and put the wheat in the barn.' "

Matthew 12: 46–50; 13: 1–30; Mark 3: 34; 4: 1–20; Luke 8: 4–21.

Let Your Light Shine

Then he asked them, "When someone lights a lamp, does he put a box over it to shut out the light? Of course not! Who ever heard of someone lighting a lamp and then covering it up to keep it from shining? No, lamps are mounted in the open, placed on a stand to shine and be useful, where they can be seen. All that is now hidden will someday come to light.

"If you have ears, listen! And be sure to put into practice what you hear. The more you do this, the more you will understand what I tell you. To him who has shall be given; from him who has not shall be taken away even what he has.

"Here is another story illustrating what the Kingdom of God is like: A farmer sowed his field, and went away, and as the days went by, the seeds grew and grew without his help. For the soil made the seeds grow. First a leaf-blade pushed through, and later the wheat-heads formed and finally the grain ripened, and then the farmer came at once with his sickle and harvested it."

Mark 4: 21, 29; Luke 8: 16.

6 Truth

Hidden Treasure and Other Illustrations

Here is another of Jesus' illustrations: "How can I describe the Kingdom of God? What story shall I use to illustrate it? A mustard seed is the smallest of all seeds, yet it grows to become one of the largest of plants. A tiny mustard seed planted in a garden grows into a tree with long branches, where birds can come and build their nests and be sheltered."

He began teaching them again about the Kingdom of God: "What is the Kingdom like?" he asked. "The Kingdom of Heaven can be compared to a woman making bread. She takes a measure of flour and mixes in the yeast until it permeates every part of the dough." Jesus constantly used these illustrations when speaking to the crowds.

Then, leaving the crowds outside, he went into the house. His disciples asked him to explain to them the illustration of the thistles and the wheat. "All right," he said, "I am the farmer who sows the choice seed. The field is the world, and the seed represents the people of the Kingdom; the thistles are the people belonging to Satan. The enemy who sowed the thistles among the wheat is the devil; the harvest is the end of the world, and the reapers are the angels.

"Just as in this story the thistles are separated and burned, so shall it be at the end of the world: I will send my angels and they will separate out of the Kingdom every temptation and all who are evil, and throw them into the furnace and burn them. There shall be weeping and gnashing of teeth. Then the godly shall shine as the sun in their Father's Kingdom.

Hidden Treasure and Other Illustrations

"Let those with ears, listen!

"The Kingdom of Heaven is like a treasure a man discovered in a field. In his excitement, he sold everything he owned to get enough money to buy the field—and get the treasure, too! Again, the Kingdom of Heaven is like a pearl merchant on the lookout for choice pearls. He discovered a real bargain—a pearl of great value—and sold everything he owned to purchase it! Again, the Kingdom of Heaven can be illustrated by a fisherman—he casts a net into the water and gathers in fish of every kind, valuable and worthless. When the net is full, he drags it up onto the beach and sits down and sorts out the edible ones into crates and throws the others away.

"That is the way it will be at the end of the world—the angels will come and separate the wicked people from the godly, casting the wicked into the fire; there shall be weeping and gnashing of teeth. Do you understand?"

"Yes," they said, "we do."

Then he added, "Those experts in Jewish law who are now my disciples have double treasures—from the Old Testament as well as from the New!"*

He used many such illustrations to teach the people as much as they were ready to understand. In fact, he taught only by illustrations in his public teaching, but afterwards, when he was alone with his disciples, he would explain his meaning to them.

As evening fell, Jesus got into a boat and suggested that they cross to the other side of the lake. They took him just as he was and started out. On the way across the wind began to rise. A fierce storm developed, with waves higher than the boat. The waves began to break into the boat until it was nearly full of water. Jesus was asleep at the back of the boat with his head on a cushion. The disciples wakened him, shouting, "Lord, save us! We're sinking!"

Jesus answered, "O you men of little faith! Why are you so

---

*Literally, "brings back out of his treasure things both new and old." The paraphrase is of course highly anachronistic!

frightened?" Then he stood up and rebuked the wind and waves. He said to the sea, "Quiet down!" and the wind fell, and there was a great calm! And he asked them, "Why were you so fearful? Where is your faith? Don't you even yet have confidence in me?"

The disciples just sat there, awed! "Who is this," they asked themselves, "that even the winds and the sea obey him?"

Mark 4: 30–40; Matthew 13: 31–52; Luke 13: 18, 19; 8: 22–25; Matthew 8: 23–27.

Casting Out the Demons

They arrived at the other side of the lake in the country of the Gadarenes, across from Galilee. A demon-possessed man ran out from a graveyard, just as Jesus was climbing from the boat. Homeless and naked, he lived among the tombs, and had such strength that he snapped handcuffs from his wrists and smashed shackles. No one was strong enough to control him.

Jesus spoke to the demon within the man and said, "Come out, you evil spirit."

He fell to the ground before Jesus, screaming, "What do you want with me, Jesus, Son of God Most High? Please, I beg you, oh, don't torment me!"

"What is your name?" Jesus asked the demon.

The demon replied, "Legion, for there are many of us here within this man." A herd of pigs was feeding in the distance, so the demons begged, "If you cast us out, send us into that herd of pigs."

Jesus gave them permission. "All right," Jesus told them. "Begone." The evil spirits came out and entered the hogs, and the entire herd plunged down the steep hillside into the lake and drowned.

The herdsmen fled to the nearby towns, spreading the news as they ran. The entire population came out to see Jesus. They saw the man who had been demon-possessed sitting quietly at Jesus' feet, clothed and sane! And the whole crowd was badly frightened. Everyone begged Jesus to go away and leave them alone.

Jesus returned to the boat. The man who had been demon-possessed begged to go too, but Jesus said no. "Go back to your family and tell them what a wonderful thing God has done for you. Go home to your friends," he told him, "and tell them how merciful God has been."

When Jesus had gone back by boat to the other side of the lake, crowds received him with open arms.

Mark 5: 1–21; Luke 8: 26–40; Matthew 8: 28–34.

Wonderful Healings

And now a man named Jairus, a leader of a Jewish synagogue, came and fell down at Jesus' feet and begged him to come home with him to heal his little daughter. "She is at the point of death," he said in desperation. "Please come and place your hands on her and make her live." His only child was a little girl twelve years old. Jesus and the disciples went with him, and the crowd thronged behind.

A messenger arrived from the Jairus' home with the news that the little girl was dead. "She's gone," he told her father, "there's no use troubling the Teacher now."

When Jesus heard what had happened, he said to the father, "Don't be afraid! Just trust me, and she'll be all right."

Jesus arrived at the rabbi's home and saw the noisy crowds and heard the funeral music. All was in great confusion, with unrestrained weeping and wailing. Jesus wouldn't let anyone in except Peter, James, John, and the little girl's father and mother. The home was filled with mourning people.

"Why all this weeping and commotion?" he asked. "Stop the weeping! She isn't dead; she is only asleep!" They laughed at him in derision.

He told them all to leave, and taking the little girl's father and mother and his three disciples, he went into the room where she was lying. Taking her by the hand he said to her, "Get up, little girl!" And she jumped up and walked around! Jesus told them to give her something to eat.

A woman who had been sick for twelve years and had suffered much from many doctors and had become poor from paying them, and was no better but, in fact, was worse, came up behind him and touched his clothes. For she thought to herself, "If I can just touch his clothing, I will be healed." And sure enough, as soon as she had touched him, she knew she was well!

Jesus realized at once that healing power had gone out from him, so he turned around in the crowd and asked, "Who touched me?"

Everyone denied it, and Peter said, "Master, so many are crowding against you and you ask who touched you?"

But Jesus told him, "No, it was someone who deliberately touched me, for I felt healing power go out from me. Who touched my clothes?" He kept looking around to see who it was who had done it. Then the frightened woman, trembling at the realization of what had happened to her, came and told him what she had done, why she had touched him and that now she was well. And he said to her, "Daughter, your faith has made you well; go in peace, healed of your disease."

As Jesus was leaving, two blind men followed along behind, shouting, "O Son of King David, have mercy on us."

They went right into the house where he was staying, and Jesus asked them, "Do you believe I can make you see?"

"Yes, Lord," they told him, "we do."

Then he touched their eyes and said, "Because of your faith it will happen." And suddenly they could see! Jesus sternly warned them not to tell anyone about it, but instead they spread his fame all over the town.

Luke 8: 41–56; Mark 5: 23–34; 38–43; Matthew 9: 19; 23; 27–31.

Jesus left that section of the country and returned to Nazareth, his home town. The next Sabbath he went to the synagogue to teach, and the people were astonished at his wisdom because he was just a local man like themselves.

"How is this possible?" the people exclaimed. "He's just a carpenter's son, and we know Mary his mother and his brothers —James, Joseph, Simon, and Judas. And his sisters—they all live here. How can he be so great?" And they became angry with him!

Then Jesus told them, "A prophet is honored everywhere except in his own country and among his relatives and by his own family." And so he did only a few miracles there, because of their unbelief.

Jesus traveled around through all the cities and villages of that area, teaching in the Jewish synagogues and announcing the Good News about the Kingdom. And wherever he went he healed people of every sort of illness. And what pity he felt for the crowds that came, because their problems were so great and they didn't know what to do or where to go for help. They were like sheep without a shepherd. "The harvest is so great, and the workers are so few," he told his disciples. "So pray to the one in charge of the harvesting, and ask him to recruit more workers for his harvest fields."

Mark 6: 1–4; Matthew 13: 55–58; 9: 35–38.

Instructions to Disciples

Jesus called his twelve disciples together and sent them out two by two, with power to cast out demons and to heal all diseases. He sent them to tell everyone about the coming of the Kingdom of God, with these instructions: "Don't go to the Gentiles or the Samaritans, but only to the people of Israel— God's lost sheep. Go and announce that the Kingdom of Heaven is near. Heal the sick, raise the dead, cure the lepers, and cast out demons. Give as freely as you have received!

"Don't even take along a walking stick," he instructed them, "nor food, nor money. Not even an extra coat, or shoes; for those you help should feed and care for you. Whenever you enter a city or village, search for a godly man and stay in his home until you leave for the next town—don't shift around from house to house while you are there. When you ask permission to stay, be friendly, and if it turns out to be a godly home, give it your blessing; if not, keep the blessing. Any city or home that doesn't welcome you—shake off the dust of that place from your feet as you leave, demonstrating God's anger against it. Truly, the wicked cities of Sodom and Gomorrah will be better off at Judgment Day than they.

"I am sending you out as sheep among wolves. Be as wary as serpents and harmless as doves. But beware! For you will be arrested and tried, and whipped in the synagogues. Yes, and you must stand trial before governors and kings for my sake. This will give you the opportunity to tell them about me, yes, to witness to the world. When you are arrested, don't worry about what to say at your trial, for you will be given the right words at the right time. For it won't be you doing the talking —it will be the Spirit of your heavenly Father speaking through you!

"Brother shall betray brother to death, and fathers shall betray their own children. And children shall rise against their parents and cause their deaths. Everyone shall hate you because you belong to me. But all of you who endure to the end shall be saved. When you are persecuted in one city, flee to the next! I will return before you have reached them all!

"A student is not greater than his teacher. A servant is not above his master. The student shares his teacher's fate. The servant shares his master's! And since I, the master of the household, have been called 'Satan,' how much more will you! But don't be afraid of those who threaten you. For the time is coming when the truth will be revealed: Their secret plots will become public information.

"What I tell you now in the gloom, shout abroad when daybreak comes. What I whisper in your ears, proclaim from the housetops! Don't be afraid of those who can kill only your bodies—but can't touch your souls! Fear only God who can destroy both soul and body in hell. Not one sparrow (What do they cost? Two for a penny?) can fall to the ground without your Father knowing it. And the very hairs of your head are all numbered. So don't worry! You are more valuable to him than many sparrows.

"If anyone publicly acknowledges me as his friend, I will openly acknowledge him as my friend before my father in heaven. But if anyone publicly denies me, I will openly deny him before my Father in heaven. Don't imagine that I came to bring peace to the earth! No, rather, a sword. I have come to set a man against his father, and a daughter against her mother, and a daughter-in-law against her mother-in-law—a man's worst enemies will be right in his own home! If you love your father and mother more than you love me, you are not worthy of being mine; or if you love your son or daughter more than me, you are not worthy of being mine. If you refuse to take up your cross and follow me, you are not worthy of being mine.

"If you cling to your life, you will lose it; but if you give it up for me, you will save it. Those who welcome you are welcoming me. And when they welcome me they are welcoming God who sent me. If you welcome a prophet because he is a man of God, you will be given the same reward a prophet gets. And if you welcome good and godly men because of their godliness, you will be given a reward like theirs. And, if, as my representatives, you give even a cup of cold water to a little child, you will surely be rewarded."

So the disciples began their circuit of the villages, telling everyone they met to turn from sin. And they cast out many demons, and healed many sick people, anointing them with olive oil.

Mark 6: 7–13; Luke 9:1–6; Matthew 10:5–42.

When reports of Jesus' miracles reached King Herod, the governor, he was worried and puzzled, for some were saying, "This is John the Baptist come back to life again." Herod had sent soldiers to arrest and imprison John at the demand of his wife Herodias, because John kept saying it was wrong for the king to marry Herodias, his brother Philip's wife. Herod sent one of his bodyguards to the prison to cut off John's head.

"I beheaded John," Herod said, "so who is this man about whom I hear such strange stories?" And he tried to see Jesus. The disciples came to tell Jesus and Jesus crossed over the Sea of Galilee by ship.

The apostles returned to Jesus and told him all they had done and what they had said to the people. He slipped quietly away with them toward the city of Bethsaida and went up into the hills and sat down with his disciples. Many people saw them leaving and ran on ahead along the shore and met them as they landed.

Matthew 14: 3, 12; Luke 9: 7–10; Mark 6: 17, 18, 27–33; John 6: 1–3.

5000 Fed

Jesus saw a great multitude of people climbing the hill, looking for him. Turning to Philip he asked, "Philip, where can we buy bread to feed all these people?" (He was testing Philip, for he already knew what he was going to do.)

"With what?" Philip asked. "It would take a fortune to buy food for all this crowd!"

Late in the afternoon all twelve of the disciples came and urged him to send the people away to the nearby villages and farms, to find food and lodging for the night. "For there is nothing to eat here in this deserted spot," they said. Jesus replied, "That isn't necessary—you feed them! How much food do we have? Go and find out."

Andrew, Simon Peter's brother, spoke up. "There's a youngster here with five barley loaves and a couple of fish! But what good is that with all this mob?"

"Bring them here," Jesus said. "Tell everyone to sit down on the ground in groups of about fifty each." Soon colorful groups of fifty or a hundred each were sitting on the green grassy slopes.

Jesus took the loaves, looked up into the sky and asked God's blessing on the meal, then broke the loaves apart and gave them to the disciples to place before the people. He did the same with the fish. And everyone ate until full! "Now gather the scraps," Jesus told his disciples, "so that nothing is wasted." And twelve baskets were filled with the leftovers!

(About 5,000 men were in the crowd that day, besides all the women and children.)

John 6: 5–13; Matthew 14: 16–21; Mark 6: 37–40; Luke 9: 12–14.

7 Faith

Walks on the Sea

Jesus saw that they were ready to take him by force and make him their king, so he told his disciples to get into their boat and cross to the other side of the lake while he stayed to get the people started home. Then afterwards he went up into the hills to pray. Night fell.

His disciples went out across the lake toward Capernaum. As darkness fell a gale swept down upon them, and the sea grew very rough. They were fighting heavy seas out in the middle of the lake and Jesus was alone on land. He saw that they were in serious trouble, rowing hard and struggling.

About three o'clock in the morning they saw Jesus walking toward the boat! They screamed in terror, for they thought he was a ghost. But Jesus immediately spoke. "It's all right," he said. "It is I! Don't be afraid."

Peter called to him: "Sir, if it is really you, tell me to come over to you, walking on the water."

"All right," the Lord said, "come along!" Peter walked on the water toward Jesus.

But he was terrified and began to sink. "Save me, Lord," he shouted. Jesus reached out his hand and rescued him.

"O man of little faith," Jesus said. "Why did you doubt me?" And when they had climbed back into the boat, the wind stopped.

They landed at Gennesaret.

Matthew 14: 22–32; Mark 6: 47–50; John 6: 15–19.

The next morning, back across the lake, crowds began gathering on the shore! When the people saw that Jesus wasn't there, nor his disciples, they got into the boats and went across to Capernaum to look for him.

When they found him, they said, "Sir, how did you get here?"

Jesus replied, "The truth of the matter is that you want to be with me because I fed you, not because you believe in me. But you shouldn't be so concerned about perishable things like food. No, spend your energy seeking the eternal life that I, the Messiah, can give you. For God the Father has sent me for this very purpose."

They replied, "What should we do to satisfy God?"

Jesus told them, "This is the will of God, that you believe in the one he has sent."

They replied, "You must show us more miracles if you want us to believe you are the Messiah. Give us free bread every day, like our fathers had while they journeyed through the wilderness! As the Scriptures say, 'Moses gave them bread from heaven.'"

John 6: 22–31.

The Bread of Life

Jesus said, "Moses didn't give it to them. My Father did. And now he offers you true Bread from heaven. The true Bread is a Person—the one sent by God from heaven, and he gives life to the world."

"Sir," they said, "give us that bread every day of our lives!"

Jesus replied, "I am the Bread of Life. No one coming to me will ever be hungry again. Those believing in me will never thirst. But the trouble is, as I have told you before, you haven't believed even though you have seen me. But some will come to me—those the Father has given me—and I will never, never reject them. For I have come here from heaven to do the will of God who sent me, not to have my own way. And this is the will of God, that I should not lose even one of all those he has given me, but that I should raise them to eternal life at the Last Day. For it is my Father's will that everyone who sees his Son and believes on him should have eternal life—that I should raise him at the Last Day."

Then the Jews began to murmur against him because he claimed to be the bread from heaven. "What?" they exclaimed. "Why, he is merely Jesus the son of Joseph, whose father and mother we know. What is this he is saying, that he came down from heaven?"

But Jesus replied, "Don't murmur among yourselves about my saying that. For no one can come to me unless the Father who sent me draws him to me, and at the Last Day I will cause all such to rise again from the dead. As it is written in the Scriptures, 'They shall all be taught of God.' Those the Father speaks to, who learn the truth from him, will be attracted to me. (Not that anyone actually sees the Father, for only I have seen him.)

"How earnestly I tell you this—anyone who believes in me already has eternal life! Yes, I am the Bread of Life! When your fathers in the wilderness ate bread from the skies, they all died. But the Bread from heaven gives eternal life to everyone who eats it. I am that Living Bread that came down out of heaven. Anyone eating this Bread shall live forever; this Bread is my flesh given to redeem humanity."

Then the Jews began arguing with each other about what he meant. "How can this man give us his flesh to eat?" they asked.

So Jesus said it again. "With all the earnestness I possess I tell you this: Unless you eat the flesh of the Messiah and drink his blood, you cannot have eternal life within you. But anyone who does eat my flesh and drink my blood has eternal life, and I will raise him at the Last Day. For my flesh is the true food, and my blood is the true drink. Everyone who eats my flesh and drinks my blood is in me, and I in him. I live by the power of the living Father who sent me, and in the same way those who partake of me shall live because of me! I am the true Bread from heaven; and anyone who eats this Bread shall live forever, and not die as your fathers did—though they ate bread from heaven." (He preached this sermon in the synagogue in Capernaum.)

His disciples said, "This is very hard to understand. Who can tell what he means?"

Jesus knew within himself that his disciples were complaining and said to them, "Does *this* offend you? Then what will you think if you see me, the Messiah, return to heaven again? Only the Holy Spirit gives eternal life. Those born only once, with physical birth, will never receive this gift. But now I have told you how to get this true spiritual life. But some of you don't believe me." (For Jesus knew from the beginning who didn't believe and knew the one who would betray him.) And he remarked, "That is what I meant when I said that no one can come to me unless the Father attracts him to me."

At this point many of his disciples deserted him. Then Jesus turned to the Twelve and asked, "Are you going too?" Simon Peter replied, "Master, to whom shall we go? You alone have the words that give eternal life, and we believe them and know you are the holy Son of God."

Then Jesus said, "I chose the twelve of you, and one is a devil." He was speaking of Judas, son of Simon Iscariot, one of the Twelve, who would betray him.

John 6: 32–71.

The Blind Leading the Blind

Some Jewish religious leaders noticed that some of Jesus' disciples failed to follow the usual Jewish rituals before eating. (For the Jews, especially the Pharisees, will never eat until they have sprinkled their arms to the elbows, as required by their ancient traditions. This is but one of many examples of laws and regulations they have clung to for centuries, and still follow, such as their ceremony of cleansing for pots, pans and dishes.)

The religious leaders asked Jesus, "Why don't your disciples follow our age-old customs? For they eat without first performing the washing ceremony. Why do your disciples disobey the ancient Jewish traditions?"

The Blind Leading the Blind

He replied, "And why do your traditions violate the direct commandments of God? You are simply rejecting God's laws and trampling them under your feet for the sake of tradition. For instance, Moses gave you this law from God: 'Honor your father and mother.' And he said that anyone who speaks against his father or mother must die. But you say it is perfectly all right for a man to disregard his needy parents, telling them, 'Sorry, I can't help you! For I have given to God what I could have given to you.' And so, by your man-made rule, you nullify the direct command of God to honor and care for your parents. You break the law of God in order to protect your man-made tradition. And this is only one example. There are many, many others.

"You bunch of hypocrites! Isaiah the prophet described you very well when he said, 'These people speak very prettily about the Lord but they have no love for him at all. Their worship is a farce, for they claim that God commands the people to obey their petty rules.' How right Isaiah was! For you ignore God's specific orders and substitute your own traditions."

Then Jesus called to the crowd to come and hear. "All of you listen," he said, "and try to understand.* You aren't made unholy by eating non-kosher food! It is what you *say* and *think* that makes you unclean. Your souls aren't harmed by what you eat, but by what you think and say!"

Then he went into a house to get away from the crowds, and his disciples asked him what he meant by the statement he had just made.

"Don't you understand either?" he asked. "Can't you see that what you eat won't harm your soul? Anything you eat passes through the digestive tract and out again." (By saying this he showed that every kind of food is kosher.) "Food doesn't come in contact with your heart. But evil words come from an evil heart, and defile the man who says them. For from within, out of men's hearts, come evil thoughts of lust, theft, murder, adul-

*Omitted in many of the ancient manuscripts: "If any man has ears to hear, let him hear."

tery, wanting what belongs to others, wickedness, deceit, lewdness, envy, slander, pride, and all other folly. All these vile things come from within. These are what defile; but there is no spiritual defilement from eating without first going through the ritual of ceremonial handwashing!"

Then the disciples told him, "You offended the Pharisees by that remark."

Jesus replied, "Every plant not planted by my Father shall be rooted up, so ignore them. They are blind guides leading the blind, and both will fall into a ditch."

Mark 7: 1–23; Matthew 15: 2–20.

Jesus in Tyre and Sidon

Then he left Galilee and went to the region of Tyre and Sidon, about fifty miles away. A woman from Canaan who was living there came to him, pleading, "Have mercy on me, O Lord, King David's Son! For my daughter has a demon within her, and it torments her constantly." (She was Syrophoenician—a "despised Gentile!")

Jesus gave her no reply. His disciples urged him to send her away. Jesus said, "I was sent to help the Jews—the lost sheep of Israel—not the Gentiles." He tried to keep it a secret that he was there, but couldn't.

She came again, the woman whose little girl was possessed by a demon, and pled with him, "Sir, help me!"

Jesus told her, "First I should help my own family—the Jews. It isn't right to take the children's food and throw it to the dogs."

She replied, "That's true, sir, but even the puppies under the table are given some scraps from the children's plates."

"Woman," Jesus told her, "your faith is large, and your request is granted. You have answered well. Go on home, for the demon has left her!" And her daughter was healed right then.

From Tyre he went to Sidon, then back to the Sea of Galilee by way of the Ten Towns. A deaf man with a speech impediment was brought to him. Jesus led him away from the crowd

Jesus in Tyre and Sidon

and put his fingers into the man's ears and touched the man's tongue. Then, looking up to heaven, he sighed and commanded, "Open!" Instantly the man could hear perfectly and speak plainly!

Jesus told the crowd not to spread the news, but the more he forbade them, the more they made it known.

Matthew 15: 22–28; Mark 7: 24–36.

8 Compassion

Seven Loaves, a Few Fishes

One day as another great crowd gathered, the people ran out of food again. Jesus called his disciples to discuss the situation.

"I pity these people," he said, "for they have been here three days, and have nothing left to eat. And if I send them home without feeding them, they will faint along the road! For some of them have come a long distance."

"Are we supposed to find food for them here in the desert?" his disciples scoffed.

Jesus said, "I don't want to send them away hungry or they will faint along the road. How many loaves of bread do you have?" he asked.

"Seven," they replied, "and a few small fish!"

Jesus told the crowd to sit down on the ground. Then he took the seven loaves, thanked God for them, broke them into pieces and passed them to his disciples; and the disciples placed them before the people. The few small fish Jesus also blessed and told the disciples to serve them. The whole crowd ate until they were full, and afterwards he sent them home. There were about 4,000 men, besides the women and children in the crowd that day and when the scraps were picked up after the meal, there were seven very large basketfuls left over!

Immediately after this he got into a boat with his disciples and crossed to Magadan to the region of Dalmanutha. The local Jewish leaders, the Pharisees and Sadducees, came to argue with him. "Do a miracle for us," they said. "Make something happen in the sky. Then we will believe in you."

Seven Loaves, a Few Fishes

He sighed deeply when he heard this and he said, "Certainly not. How many more miracles do you people need? You are good at reading the weather signs of the skies—red sky tonight means fair weather tomorrow; red sky in the morning means foul weather all day—but you can't read the obvious signs of the times! This evil, unbelieving nation is asking for some strange sign in the heavens, but no further proof will be given except the miracle that happened to Jonah."

He got back into the boat and crossed to the other side of the lake. But the disciples had forgotten to stock up on food before they left, and had only one loaf of bread in the boat. Jesus said to them very solemnly, "Beware of the yeast of King Herod and of the Pharisees and Sadducees."

"What does he mean?" the disciples asked each other. They finally decided that he must be talking about their forgetting to bring bread.

Jesus knew what they were thinking and told them, "O men of little faith! Why are you so worried about having no food? Can't you understand? Are your hearts too hard to take it in? Your eyes are to see with—why don't you look? Why don't you open your ears and listen? Don't you remember anything at all? Won't you ever understand?

"Don't you remember at all the 5,000 I fed with five loaves, and the basketfuls left over? Don't you remember the 4,000 I fed and all that was left? When I fed the 5,000 men with five loaves of bread, how many basketfuls of scraps did you pick up afterwards?"

"Twelve," they said.

"And when I fed the 4,000 with seven loaves, how much was left?"

"Seven basketfuls," they said.

"And yet you think I'm worried that we have no bread? How could you even think I was talking about food? But again I say, 'Beware of the yeast of the Pharisees and Sadducees.' "

When they arrived at Bethsaida, some people brought a blind man to him. Jesus took the blind man by the hand and led him

out of the village, and laid his hands over his eyes. "Can yo
see anything now?" Jesus asked him.

The man looked around. "Yes!" he said, "I see men! But
can't see them very clearly; they look like tree trunks walkin
around!"

Jesus placed his hands over the man's eyes again and as th
man stared intently, his sight was completely restored, and h
saw everything clearly, drinking in the sights around him. Jesu
sent him home to his family. "Don't even go back to the villag
first," he said.

Mark 8: 1–26; Matthew 15: 32, 34, 39; 16: 1–1

Peter the Rock

Jesus and his disciples came to the villages of Caesarea Phi
lippi. As they were walking along he asked them, "Who do th
people think I am? What are they saying about me?"

"Some of them think you are John the Baptist," the disciple
replied, "and others say you are Elijah or Jeremiah or one of th
other ancient prophets risen from the dead."

Then he asked them, "Who do you think I am?"

Simon Peter answered, "The Christ of God."

"God has blessed you, Simon, son of Jonah," Jesus said, "fc
my Father in heaven has personally revealed this to you—th
is not from any human source. You are Peter, a stone; and upo
this rock I will build my church; and all the powers of hell sha
not prevail against it. And I will give you the keys of th
Kingdom of Heaven; whatever doors you lock on earth shall k
locked in heaven; and whatever doors you open on earth sha
be open in heaven!"

Then he warned the disciples against telling others that h
was the Messiah. From then on Jesus began to speak plainly t
his disciples about his going to Jerusalem, and that he would k
killed. "For I, the Messiah, must suffer much," he said, "and k
rejected by the Jewish leaders—the elders, chief priests, an
teachers of the Law—and be killed; and three days later I wi
come back to life again!" He talked about it quite frankly wit
them.

74

Peter chided him. "Heaven forbid, sir," he said. "This is not going to happen to you!"

Jesus turned and looked at his disciples and then said to Peter very sternly, "Satan, get behind me! You are a dangerous trap to me. You are looking at this only from a human point of view and not from God's."

Then he called his disciples and the crowds to come over and listen. He said to all, "Anyone who wants to follow me must put aside his own desires and conveniences and carry his cross with him every day and *keep close to me!* Whoever loses his life for my sake will save it, but whoever insists on keeping his life will lose it. What profit is there, how does a man benefit if he gains the whole world and loses his soul in the process? For is anything worth more than his soul?

"For I, the Son of Mankind, shall come with my angels in the glory of my Father and judge each person according to his deeds. Anyone who is ashamed of me and my message in these days of unbelief and sin, I, The Messiah, will be ashamed of him when I return in my glory and in the glory of the Father and the holy angels. But this is the simple truth—some of you who are standing here right now will not die until you have seen the Kingdom of God arrive in great power, will certainly live to see me coming in my Kingdom."

Matthew 16: 14–28; Mark 8: 27–38; 9: 1; Luke 9: 19–27.

Jesus Transfigured

Eight days later Jesus took Peter, James, and John, his brother, with him to the top of a high and lonely hill to pray. No one else was there. As he was praying, his face began to shine with glory like the sun and his clothing became dazzling white and blazed with light, far more glorious than any earthly process could ever make it!

Then two men appeared and began talking with him—Moses and Elijah! They were splendid in appearance, glorious to see; and they were speaking of his death at Jerusalem, to be carried out in accordance with God's plan.

Peter and the others saw Jesus covered with brightness and

glory, and the two men standing with him. A bright cloud formed above them and covered them; and a voice from the cloud said, *"This* is my beloved Son, and I am wonderfully pleased with him. Obey *him."*

The disciples fell face downward to the ground, terribly frightened. Jesus came and touched them. "Get up," he said, "don't be afraid." Suddenly when they looked around, Moses and Elijah were gone, and only Jesus was with them.

Jesus commanded them not to tell anyone what they had seen until after he had risen from the dead. They wondered what he meant by "rising from the dead."

His disciples asked, "Why do the Jewish leaders insist Elijah must return before the Messiah comes?"

Jesus replied, "They are right." He agreed that Elijah must come first and prepare the way—and that he had, in fact, already come, but he wasn't recognized, and was badly mistreated, just as the prophets had predicted. "And I, the Messiah, shall also suffer at their hands and be treated with utter contempt."

Then the disciples realized he was speaking of John the Baptist. They didn't tell anyone what they had seen until long afterwards.

At the bottom of the mountain they found a great crowd surrounding the other nine disciples, as some Jewish leaders argued with them. "What's all the argument about?" Jesus asked.

One of the men in the crowd spoke up and said, "Teacher, I brought my son for you to heal. Sir, have mercy, for he is mentally deranged, and in great trouble, for he often falls into the fire or into the water. A demon keeps seizing him so that he foams at the mouth, and grinds his teeth and becomes rigid. I brought him to your disciples, but they couldn't cure him. This boy is my only son."

Jesus replied, "Oh, you stubborn, faithless people! How long shall I bear with you? Bring him here to me." They brought the boy, and as he was coming the demon convulsed the child horribly, and he fell to the ground writhing and foaming at the mouth.

"How long has he been this way?" Jesus asked the father.

He replied, "Since he was very small. Have mercy on us."

Jesus said, *"Anything* is possible if you have faith."

The father instantly replied, "I *do* have faith; oh, help me to have *more!"*

Jesus rebuked the demon. "O demon of deafness and dumbness," he said, "I command you to come out of this child and enter him no more." From that moment the boy was well.

Luke 9: 28–42; Matthew 17: 1–18; Mark 9: 2–25.

A Grain of Mustard Seed

When Jesus was alone in the house with his disciples, they asked him, "Why couldn't we cast that demon out?" Jesus replied: "Because of your little faith. For if you had faith even as small as a tiny mustard seed you could say to this mountain, 'Move!' and it would go. Nothing would be impossible. But this kind of demon won't leave unless you have prayed and gone without food."

Mark 9: 28, 29; Matthew 17: 20, 21.

Who Welcomes a Little Child, Welcomes Me

Leaving that region Jesus traveled through Galilee. While in Galilee the people exclaimed over the things he was doing. As they were exclaiming, Jesus said to his disciples, "Listen to me and remember what I say. I, the Messiah, am going to be betrayed into the power of those who will kill me, and on the third day afterwards I will be brought back to life again." But the disciples didn't know what he meant.

Now came an argument among the disciples. On the road to Capernaum they were arguing about which of them was the greatest. When they were settled in the house, Jesus asked them, "What were you discussing out on the road?" But they were ashamed to answer. Jesus knew their thoughts and said, "Anyone wanting to be the greatest must be the least—the servant of all!" He placed a little child in his arms and said, "Anyone who welcomes a little child like this in my name is welcoming me, and anyone who welcomes me is welcoming my Father who sent me! Your care for others is the measure of your greatness."

On their arrival in Capernaum, the Temple tax collectors came to Peter and asked him, "Doesn't your master pay taxes?"

"Of course he does," Peter replied.

Then he went into the house to talk to Jesus about it, but before he had a chance to speak, Jesus asked him, "What do you think, Peter? Do kings levy assessments against their own people, or against conquered foreigners?"

"Against the foreigners," Peter replied.

"Well, then," Jesus said, "the citizens are free! However, we don't want to offend them, so go down to the shore and throw in a line, and open the mouth of the first fish you catch. You will find a coin to cover the taxes for both of us; take it and pay them."

John said, "Master, we saw someone using your name to cast out demons. And we told him not to. After all, he isn't in our group."

"Don't forbid him!" Jesus said. "For no one doing miracles in my name will quickly turn against me. Anyone who isn't against us is for us.

"If anyone so much as gives you a cup of water because you are Christ's—I say this solemnly—he won't lose his reward.

"But if someone causes one of these little ones who believe in me to lose faith—it would be better for that man if a huge millstone were tied around his neck and he were thrown into the sea.

"If your hand does wrong, cut it off. Better live forever with one hand than be thrown into the unquenchable fires of hell with two!

"If your foot carries you toward evil, cut it off! Better be lame and live forever than have two feet that carry you to hell.

"And if your eye is sinful, gouge it out. Better enter the Kingdom of God half blind than have two eyes and see the fires of hell, where the worm never dies, and the fire never goes out —where all are salted with fire.

"Good salt is worthless if it loses its saltiness; it can't season anything. So don't lose your flavor! Live in peace with each other."

Mark 9: 30–50; Luke 9: 43–50; Matthew 17: 22–27.

Genius of the Childlike

About that time the disciples came to Jesus to ask which of them would be greatest in the Kingdom of Heaven! Jesus called a small child over to him and set the little fellow down among them, and said, "Unless you turn to God from your sins and become as little children, you will never get into the Kingdom of Heaven. Therefore anyone who humbles himself as this little child, is the greatest in the Kingdom of Heaven. And any of you who welcomes a little child like this because you are mine, is welcoming me and caring for me. But if any of you causes one of these little ones who trusts in me to lose his faith, it would be better for you to have a rock tied to your neck and be thrown into the sea.

"Woe upon the world for all of its evils. Temptation to do wrong is inevitable, but woe to the man who does the tempting. So if your hand or foot causes you to sin, cut it off and throw it away. Better to enter heaven crippled than to be in hell with both of your hands and feet. And if your eye causes you to sin, gouge it out and throw it away. Better to enter heaven with one eye than to be in hell with two.

"Beware that you don't look down upon a single one of these little children. For I tell you that in heaven their angels have constant access to my Father. And I, the Messiah, came to save the lost."

Matthew 18: 1–11.

The Lost Sheep

"If a man has a hundred sheep, and one wanders away and is lost, what will he do? Won't he leave the ninety-nine others and go out into the hills to search for the lost one? And if he finds it, he will rejoice over it more than over the ninety-nine others safe at home! Just so, it is not my Father's will that even one of these little ones should perish.

"If a brother sins against you, go to him privately and confront him with his fault. If he listens and confesses it, you have won back a brother. But if not, then take one or two others with you and go back to him again, proving everything you say by these witnesses. If he still refuses to listen, then take your case to the church, and if the church's verdict favors you, but he won't accept it, then the church should excommunicate him.

"And I tell you this—whatever you bind on earth is bound in heaven, and whatever you free on earth will be freed in heaven.

"I also tell you this—if two of you agree down here on earth concerning anything you ask for, my Father in heaven will do it for you. For where two or three gather together because they are mine, I will be right there among them."

Then Peter came to him and asked, "Sir, how often should I forgive a brother who sins against me? Seven times?"

"No!" Jesus replied, "seventy times seven!

"The Kingdom of Heaven can be compared to a king who decided to bring his accounts up to date. In the process, one of his debtors was brought in who owed him $10,000,000!* He couldn't pay, so the king ordered him sold for the debt, also his wife and children and everything he had. But the man fell down before the king, his face in the dust, and said, 'Oh, sir, be patient with me and I will pay it all.' Then the king was filled with pity for him and released him and forgave his debt.

"But when the man left the king, he went to a man who owed him $2,000 and grabbed him by the throat and demanded instant payment. The man fell down before him and begged him to give him a little time. 'Be patient and I will pay it,' he pled. But his creditor wouldn't wait. He had the man arrested and jailed until the debt would be paid in full.

"Then the man's friends went to the king and told him what

*Literally, "10,000 talents."

had happened. And the king called before him the man he had forgiven and said, 'You evil-hearted wretch! Here I forgave you all that tremendous debt, just because you asked me to—shouldn't you have mercy on others, just as I had mercy on you?

"Then the angry king sent the man to the torture chamber until he had paid every last penny due. So shall my heavenly Father do to you if you refuse to truly forgive your brothers."

Matthew 18: 12-35.

The Feast of the Tabernacle

After this, Jesus went to Galilee, going from village to village, for he wanted to stay out of Judea where the Jewish leaders were plotting his death.

But soon it was time for the Tabernacle Ceremonies, one of the annual Jewish holidays, and Jesus' brothers urged him to go to Judea for the celebration. "Go where more people can see your miracles!" they scoffed. "You can't be famous when you hide like this! If you're so great, prove it to the world!" For even his brothers didn't believe in him.

Jesus replied, "It is not the right time for me to go now. But you can go anytime and it will make no difference, for the world can't hate you; but it does hate me, because I accuse it of sin and evil. You go on, it is not the right time for me." So he remained in Galilee.

But after his brothers had left for the celebration, then he went too, though secretly, staying out of the public eye.

There was a lot of discussion about him among the crowds. Some said, "He's a wonderful man," while others said, "No, he's duping the public." But no one had the courage to speak out for him in public for fear of reprisals from the Jewish leaders.

The Jewish leaders tried to find him at the celebration. Then, midway through the festival, Jesus went up to the Temple and preached openly. The Jewish leaders were surprised when they heard him. "How can he know so much when he's never been to our schools?" they asked.

So Jesus told them, "I'm not teaching you my own thoughts,

but those of God who sent me. If any of you really determines to do God's will, then you will certainly know whether my teaching is from God or is merely my own. Anyone presenting his own ideas is looking for praise for himself, but anyone seeking to honor the one who sent him is a good and true person. None of *you* obeys the laws of Moses! So why pick on *me* for breaking them? Why kill *me* for this?"

The crowd replied, "Who's trying to kill you? You're out of your mind!"

Jesus replied, "I worked on the Sabbath by healing a man, and you were surprised. But you work on the Sabbath, too, whenever you obey Moses' law of circumcision (actually, however, this tradition of circumcision is older than the Mosaic law); for if the correct time for circumcising your children falls on the Sabbath, you go ahead and do it, as you should. So why should I be condemned for making a man completely well on the Sabbath?

"Think this through and you will see that I am right."

Some of the people who lived there in Jerusalem said among themselves, "Isn't this the man they are trying to kill? But here he is preaching in public, and they say nothing to him. Can it be that our leaders have learned, after all, that he really is the Messiah? But how could he be? For we know where this man was born; when Christ comes, he will just appear and no one will know where he comes from."

So Jesus, in a sermon in the Temple, called out, "Yes, you know me and where I was born and raised, but I am the representative of one you don't know, and he is Truth. I know him because I was with him, and he sent me to you."

Then the Jewish leaders sought to arrest him; but God's time had not yet come. Many believed on him. "After all," they said, "what miracles do you expect the Messiah to do that this man hasn't done?"

When the Pharisees heard that the crowds were in this mood, they and the chief priests sent officers to arrest Jesus. But Jesus told them, "Not yet! I am to be here a little longer. Then I shall return to the one who sent me. You will search for me but not find me. And you won't be able to come where I am!"

The Jewish leaders were puzzled by this statement. They asked, "What does he mean about our looking for him and not being able to find him, and, 'You won't be able to come where I am'?"

On the last day, the climax of the holidays, Jesus shouted to the crowds, "If anyone is thirsty, let him come to me and drink. For the Scriptures declare that rivers of living water shall flow from the inmost being of anyone who believes in me." (He was speaking of the Holy Spirit, who would be given to everyone believing in him.)

When the crowds heard him say this, some of them declared, "This man surely is the prophet who will come just before the Messiah." Others said, "He *is* the Messiah." Still others, "But he *can't* be! Will the Messiah come from *Galilee?*"

So the crowd was divided about him. And some wanted him arrested, but no one touched him. The Temple police who had been sent to arrest him returned to the chief priests and Pharisees. "Why didn't you bring him in?" they demanded.

"He says such wonderful things!" they mumbled. "We've never heard anything like it."

Everybody went home. Jesus returned to the Mount of Olives.

John 7: 1–46, 53; 8: 1.

Jesus Rebukes the Jewish Leaders

Early the next morning Jesus was back again at the Temple. A crowd soon gathered, and he sat down and talked to them. As he was speaking, the Jewish leaders and Pharisees brought a woman caught in adultery and placed her out in front of the staring crowd.

"Teacher," they said to Jesus, "Moses' law says to kill her. What about it?" They were trying to trap him into saying something they could use against him.

But Jesus stooped down and wrote in the dust with his finger.

83

They kept demanding an answer, so he stood up again and said, "All right, hurl the stones at her until she dies. But only he who never sinned may throw the first!"

Then he stooped down again and wrote some more in the dust. And the Jewish leaders slipped away one by one, beginning with the eldest, until only Jesus was left in front of the crowd with the woman.

Then Jesus stood up again and said to her, "Where are your accusers? Didn't even one of them condemn you?"

"No, sir," she said.

And Jesus said, "Neither do I. Go and sin no more."

Later, in one of his talks, Jesus said to the people, "I am the Light of the world. So if you follow me, you won't be stumbling through the darkness, for living light will flood your path."

The Pharisees replied, "You are boasting—and lying!"

Jesus told them, "These claims are true even though I make them concerning myself. For I know where I came from and where I am going, but you don't know this about me. You pass judgment on me without knowing the facts. I am not judging you now; but if I were, it would be an absolutely correct judgment in every respect, for I have with me the Father who sent me.

"Your laws say that if two men agree on something that has happened, their witness is accepted as fact. Well, I am one witness, and my Father who sent me is the other."

"Where is your father?" they asked.

Jesus answered, "You don't know who I am, so you don't know who my Father is. If you knew me, then you would know him too." Jesus made these statements while in the section of the Temple known as the Treasury. But he was not arrested, for his time had not yet run out.

Later he said to them again, "I am going away; and you will search for me, and die in your sins. And you cannot come where I am going."

The Jews asked, "Is he planning suicide? What does he mean, 'You cannot come where I am going'?"

Then he said to them, "You are from below; I am from above.

Jesus Rebukes the Jewish Leaders

You are of this world; I am not. That is why I said that you will die in your sins; for unless you believe that I am the Messiah, the Son of God, you will die in your sins."

"Tell us who you are," they demanded.

He replied, "I am the one I have always claimed to be. I could condemn you for much and teach you much, but I won't, for I say only what I am told to by the one who sent me; and he is Truth."

But they still didn't understand that he was talking to them about God.

So Jesus said, "When you have killed the Messiah, then you will realize that I am he and that I have not been telling you my own ideas, but have spoken what the Father taught me. And he who sent me is with me—he has not deserted me—for I always do those things that are pleasing to him."

Then many of the Jewish leaders who heard him say these things began believing him to be the Messiah.

Jesus said to them, "You are truly my disciples if you live as I tell you to, and you will know the truth, and the truth will set you free."

"But we are descendants of Abraham," they said, "and have never been slaves to any man on earth! What do you mean, 'set free'?"

Jesus replied, "You are slaves of sin, every one of you. And slaves don't have rights, but the Son has every right there is! So if the Son sets you free, you will indeed be free—(Yes, I realize that you are descendants of Abraham!) And yet some of you are trying to kill me because my message does not find a home within your hearts. I am telling you what I saw when I was with my Father. But you are following the advice of *your* father."

"Our father is Abraham," they declared.

Jesus replied, "No, for if he were, you would follow his good example. But instead you are trying to kill me—and all because I told you the truth I heard from God. Abraham wouldn't do a thing like that! No, you are obeying your *real* father when you act that way."

They replied, "We were not born out of wedlock—our true Father is God himself."

Jesus told them, "If that were so, then you would love me, for I have come to you from God. I am not here on my own, but he sent me.

"Why can't you understand what I am saying? It is because you are prevented from doing so! For you are the children of your father the devil and you love to do the evil things he does. He was a murderer from the beginning and a hater of truth— there is not an iota of truth in him. When he lies, it is perfectly normal; for he is the father of liars.

"And so when I tell the truth, you just naturally don't believe it! Which of you can truthfully accuse me of one single sin? No one! And since I am telling you the truth, why don't you believe me? Anyone whose Father is God listens gladly to the words of God. Since you don't, it proves you aren't his children."

"You Samaritan! Foreigner! Devil!" the Jewish leaders snarled. "Didn't we say all along you were possessed by a demon?"

Jesus said, "No, I have no demon in me. For I honor my Father —and you dishonor me. And though I have no wish to make myself great, God wants this for me and judges those who reject me. With all the earnestness I have I tell you this—no one who obeys me shall ever die!"

The leaders of the Jews said, "Now we know you are possessed by a demon. Even Abraham and the mightiest prophets died, and yet you say that obeying you will keep a man from dying! So you are greater than our father Abraham, who died? And greater than the prophets, who died? Who do you think you are?"

Then Jesus told them this: "If I am merely boasting about myself, it doesn't count. But it is my Father—and you claim him as your God—who is saying these glorious things about me. But you do not even know him. I do. If I said otherwise, I would be as great a liar as you! But it is true—I know him and fully obey him. Your father Abraham rejoiced to see my day. He knew I was coming and was glad."

Healing of Man Born Blind

The Jewish leaders: "You aren't even fifty years old—sure, you've seen Abraham!"

Jesus: "The absolute truth is that I was in existence before Abraham was ever born!"

At that point the Jewish leaders picked up stones to kill him. But Jesus was hidden from them, and walked past them and left the Temple.

John 8: 2–59.

Healing of Man Born Blind

As Jesus was walking along, he saw a man blind from birth.

"Master," his disciples asked him, "why was this man born blind? Was it a result of his own sins or those of his parents?"

"Neither," Jesus answered. "But to demonstrate the power of God. All of us must quickly carry out the tasks assigned us by the one who sent me, for there is little time left before the night falls and all work comes to an end. But while I am still here in the world, I give it my light."

Then he smoothed mud over the blind man's eyes, and told him, "Go and wash in the Pool of Siloam." The man went and washed and came back seeing!

His neighbors asked, "Is this the same fellow—that beggar?"

The beggar said, "I *am* the same man!"

Then they asked him how in the world he could see. What had happened? He told them, "A man they call Jesus made mud and smoothed it over my eyes and told me to go to the Pool of Siloam and wash off the mud. I did, and I can see!"

All this occurred on a Sabbath.

The Pharisees then said, "Then this fellow Jesus is not from God, because he is working on the Sabbath." Others said, "But how could an ordinary sinner do such miracles?" So there was a deep division of opinion among them.

The Jewish leaders called in his parents and asked them, "Is this your son? Was he born blind? If so, how can he see?"

His parents replied, "We know this is our son and that he was born blind, but we don't know what happened to make him see. He is old enough to speak for himself. Ask him." They said this

87

in fear of the Jewish leaders who had announced that anyone saying Jesus was the Messiah would be excommunicated.

So for the second time they called in the man who had been blind and told him, "Give the glory to God, not to Jesus, for we know Jesus is an evil person. We don't know anything about him."

"Why, that's very strange!" the man replied. "He can heal blind men, and yet you don't know anything about him! Well, God doesn't listen to evil men, but he has open ears to those who worship him and do his will. If this man were not from God, he couldn't do it."

"You illegitimate bastard, you!" they shouted. "Are you trying to teach *us?*" And they threw him out.

When Jesus heard what had happened, he found the man and said, "Do you believe in the Messiah?"

The man answered, "Who is he, sir, for I want to."

"You have seen him," Jesus said, "and he is speaking to you!"

"Yes, Lord," the man said, "I believe!"

Jesus told him, "I have come into the world to give sight to those who are spiritually blind and to show those who think they see that they are blind."

The Pharisees who were standing there asked, "Are you saying we are blind?"

"If you were blind, you wouldn't be guilty," Jesus replied. "But your guilt remains because you claim to know what you are doing."

John 9: 1–41.

The Abundant Life

"Anyone refusing to walk through the gate into a sheepfold, who sneaks over the wall, must surely be a thief! For a shepherd comes through the gate. The gatekeeper opens the gate for him, and the sheep hear his voice and come to him; and he calls his own sheep by name and leads them out.

"He walks ahead of them; and they follow him, for they recognize his voice. They won't follow a stranger but will run from him, for they don't recognize his voice."

Those who heard Jesus use this illustration didn't understand what he meant, so he explained it to them. "I am the Gate for the sheep," he said. "All others who came before me were thieves and robbers. But the true sheep did not listen to them. Yes, I am the Gate. Those who come in by way of the Gate will be saved and will go in and out and find green pastures.

"The thief's purpose is to steal, kill and destroy. My purpose is to give life in all its fullness.

"I am the Good Shepherd. The Good Shepherd lays down his life for the sheep. A hired man will run when he sees a wolf coming and will leave the sheep, for they aren't his and he isn't their shepherd. And so the wolf leaps on them and scatters the flock. The hired man runs because he is hired and has no real concern for the sheep. I am the Good Shepherd and know my own sheep, and they know me, just as my Father knows me and I know the Father; and I lay down my life for the sheep.

"I have other sheep, too, in another fold. I must bring them also, and they will heed my voice; and there will be one flock with one Shepherd.

"The Father loves me because I lay down my life that I may have it back again. No one can kill me without my consent— I lay down my life voluntarily. For I have the right and power to lay it down when I want to and also the right and power to take it again. For the Father has given me this right."

It was winter, and Jesus was in Jerusalem at the time of the Dedication Celebration. He was at the Temple, walking through the section known as Solomon's Hall.

The Jewish leaders surrounded him and asked, "How long are you going to keep us in suspense? If you are the Messiah, tell us plainly."

"I have already told you, and you don't believe me," Jesus replied. "The proof is in the miracles I do in the name of my Father. But you don't believe me because you are not part of my flock. My sheep recognize my voice, and I know them, and they follow me. I give them eternal life and they shall never perish.

No one shall snatch them away from me.

"My Father has given them to me, and he is more powerful than anyone else, so no one can kidnap them from me. I and the Father are one."

Then again the Jewish leaders picked up stones to kill him.

Jesus said, "At God's direction I have done many a miracle to help the people. For which one are you killing me?"

They replied, "Not for any good work, but for blasphemy; you, a mere man, have declared yourself to be God."

"In your own Law it says that men are gods!" he replied. "So if the Scripture, which cannot be untrue, speaks of those as gods to whom the message of God came, do you call it blasphemy when the one sanctified and sent into the world by the Father says, 'I am the Son of God'?

"Don't believe me unless I do miracles of God. But if I do, believe them even if you don't believe me. Then you will become convinced that the Father is in me, and I in the Father."

Once again they started to arrest him. But he walked away and left them, and went beyond the Jordan River to stay near the place where John was first baptizing.

John 10: 1–18; 22–40.

9 Fidelity

The Seventy Disciples

As the time drew near for his return to heaven, Jesus moved steadily onward towards Jerusalem with an iron will. He sent messengers ahead to reserve rooms for them in a Samaritan village. But they were turned away! James and John said to Jesus, "Master, shall we order fire down from heaven to burn them up?" But Jesus rebuked them, and they went on to another village.

As they were walking along someone said to Jesus, "I will always follow you no matter where you go."

But Jesus replied, "Remember, I don't even own a place to lay my head. Foxes have dens to live in, and birds have nests, but I, the Messiah, have no earthly home at all."

Another time, when he invited a man to come with him and to be his disciple, the man agreed—but wanted to wait until his father's death. Jesus replied, "Let those without eternal life concern themselves with things like that. Your duty is to come and preach the coming of the Kingdom of God to all the world."

Another said, "Yes, Lord, I will come, but first let me ask permission of those at home."

But Jesus told him, "Anyone who lets himself be distracted from the work I plan for him is not fit for the Kingdom of God."

The Lord now chose seventy other disciples and sent them on ahead in pairs to all the towns and villages he planned to visit later. These were his instructions to them: "Plead with the Lord of the harvest to send out more laborers to help you, for the harvest is so plentiful and the workers so few. Go now, and remember that I am sending you out as lambs among wolves. Don't take any money with you, or a beggar's bag, or even an extra pair of shoes. And don't waste time along the way. Whenever you enter a home, give it your blessing. If it is worthy of the blessing, the blessing will stand; if not, the blessing will return to you.

"When you enter a village, don't shift around from home to home, but stay in one place, eating and drinking without question whatever is set before you. And don't hesitate to accept hospitality, for the workman is worthy of his wages! If a town welcomes you, follow these two rules:

"1. Eat whatever is set before you.

"2. Heal the sick; and as you heal them, say, 'The Kingdom of God is very near you now.'

"But if a town refuses you, go out into its streets and say, 'We wipe the dust of your town from our feet as a public announcement of your doom. Never forget how close you were to the Kingdom of God!' Even wicked Sodom will be better off than such a city on the Judgment Day. What horrors await you, you cities of Chorazin and Bethsaida! For if the miracles I did for you had been done in the cities of Tyre and Sidon, their people would have sat in deep repentance long ago, clothed in sackcloth and throwing ashes on their heads to show their remorse. Yes, Tyre and Sidon will receive less punishment on the Judgment Day than you.

"And you people of Capernaum, what shall I say about you? Will you be exalted to heaven? No, you shall be brought down to hell." Then he said to the disciples, "Those who welcome you are welcoming me. And those who reject you are rejecting me. And those who reject me are rejecting God who sent me."

When the seventy disciples returned, they joyfully reported to him, "Even the demons obey us when we use your name."

"Yes," he told them, "I saw Satan falling from heaven as a flash of lightning! And I have given you authority over all the power of the Enemy, and to walk among serpents and scorpions and to crush them. Nothing shall injure you! However, the important thing is not that demons obey you, but that your names are registered as citizens of heaven."

Then he was filled with the joy of the Holy Spirit and said, "I praise you, O Father, Lord of heaven and earth, for hiding these things from the intellectuals and worldly wise and for revealing them to those who are as trusting as little children. Yes, thank you, Father, for that is the way you wanted it. I am the Agent of my Father in everything; and no one really knows the Son except the Father, and no one really knows the Father except the Son and those to whom the Son chooses to reveal him."

Then, turning to the twelve disciples, he said quietly, "How privileged you are to see what you have seen. Many a prophet and king of old has longed for these days, to see and hear what you have seen and heard."

Luke 9: 51–62; 10: 1–24.

Importance of Love and Mercy

One day an expert on Moses' laws came to test Jesus' orthodoxy by asking him this question: "Teacher, what does a man need to do to live forever in heaven?"

Jesus replied, "What does Moses' law say about it?"

"It says," he replied, "that you must love the Lord your God with all your heart, and with all your soul, and with all your strength, and with all your mind. And you must love your neighbor just as much as you love yourself."

"Right!" Jesus told him. "Do this and you shall live!"

The man wanted to justify (his lack of love for some kinds of people), so he asked, "Which neighbors?"

Jesus replied with an illustration: "A Jew going on a trip from Jerusalem to Jericho was attacked by bandits. They stripped him of his clothes and money and beat him up and left him lying half dead beside the road.

By chance a Jewish priest came along; and when he saw the man lying there, he crossed to the other side of the road and passed him by.

93

A Jewish Temple-assistant walked over and looked at him lying there, but then went on.

But a despised Samaritan came along, and when he saw him, he felt deep pity. Kneeling beside him the Samaritan soothed his wounds with medicine and bandaged them. Then he put the man on his donkey and walked along beside him till they came to an inn, where he nursed him through the night. The next day he handed the innkeeper two twenty-dollar bills* and told him to take care of the man. 'If his bill runs higher than that,' he said, 'I'll pay the difference the next time I am here.'

"Now which of these three would you say was a neighbor to the bandits' victim?"

The man replied, "The one who showed him some pity."

Then Jesus said, "Yes, now go and do the same."

Luke 10: 25–37.

He Teaches Them to Pray

When Jesus had been out praying, one of his disciples came to him as he finished and said, "Lord, teach us a prayer to recite just as John taught one to his disciples." And this is the prayer he taught them: "Father, may your name be honored for its holiness; send your Kingdom soon. Give us our food day by day. And forgive our sins—for we have forgiven those who sinned against us. And don't allow us to be tempted."

Then, teaching them more about prayer, he used this illustration: "Suppose you went to a friend's house at midnight, wanting to borrow three loaves of bread. You would shout up to him, 'A friend of mine has just arrived for a visit and I've nothing to give him to eat.' He would call down from his bedroom, 'Please don't ask me to get up. The door is locked for the night and we are all in bed. I just can't help you this time.' But I'll tell you this—though he won't do it as a friend, if you keep knocking long enough he will get up and give you everything you want—just because of your persistence. And so it is with

*Literally, "two denarii," each the equivalent of a modern day's wage.

prayer—keep on asking and you will keep on getting; keep on looking and you will keep on finding; knock and the door will be opened. Everyone who asks, receives; all who seek, find; and the door is opened to everyone who knocks.

"You men who are fathers—if your boy asks for bread, do you give him a stone? If he asks for fish, do you give him a snake? If he asks for an egg, do you give him a scorpion? Of course not! And if even sinful persons like yourselves give children what they need, don't you realize that your heavenly Father will do at least as much, and give the Holy Spirit to those who ask for him?"

As he was speaking, a woman in the crowd called out, "God bless your mother—the womb from which you came, and the breasts that gave you suck!"

He replied, "Yes, but even more blessed are all who hear the Word of God and put it into practice."

As the crowd pressed in upon him, he preached them this sermon: "These are evil times, with evil people. They keep asking for some strange happening in the skies to prove I am the Messiah, but the only proof I will give them is a miracle like that of Jonah, whose experiences proved to the people of Nineveh that God had sent him. My similar experience will prove that God has sent me to these people.

"And at the Judgment Day the Queen of Sheba shall arise and point her finger at this generation, condemning it, for she went on a long, hard journey to listen to the wisdom of Solomon; but one far greater than Solomon is here and few pay any attention.

"The men of Nineveh, too, shall arise and condemn this nation, for they repented at the preaching of Jonah; and someone far greater than Jonah is here but this nation won't listen.

"No one lights a lamp and hides it! Instead, he puts it on a lampstand to give light to all who enter the room. Your eyes light up your inward being. A pure eye lets sunshine into your soul. A lustful eye shuts out the light and plunges you into darkness. So watch out that the sunshine isn't blotted out. If you are filled with light within, with no dark corners, then your face will be radiant too, as though a floodlight is beamed upon you."

As he was speaking, one of the Pharisees asked him home for a meal. When Jesus arrived, he sat down to eat without first performing the ceremonial washing required by Jewish custom. This greatly surprised his host. Then Jesus said to him, "You Pharisees wash the outside, but inside you are still dirty—full of greed and wickedness! Fools! Didn't God make the inside as well as the outside? Purity is best demonstrated by generosity. But woe to you Pharisees! For though you are careful to tithe even the smallest part of your income, you completely forget about justice and the love of God. You should tithe, yes, but you should not leave these other things undone. Woe to you Pharisees! For how you love the seats of honor in the synagogues and the respectful greetings from everyone as you walk through the markets! Yes, awesome judgment is awaiting you. For you are like hidden graves in a field. Men go by you with no knowledge of the corruption they are passing.

"Sir," said an expert in religious law who was standing there, "you have insulted my profession, too, in what you just said."

"Yes," said Jesus, "the same horrors await you! For you crush men beneath impossible religious demands—demands that you yourselves would never think of trying to keep.

"Woe to you! For you are exactly like your ancestors who killed the prophets long ago. Murderers! You agree with your fathers that what they did was right—you would have done the same yourselves. This is what God says about you: 'I will send prophets and apostles to you, and you will kill some of them and chase away the others.' And you of this generation will be held responsible for the murder of God's servants from the founding of the world—from the murder of Abel to the murder of Zechariah who perished between the altar and the sanctuary. Yes, it will surely be charged against you.

"Woe to you experts in religion! For you hide the truth from the people. You won't accept it for yourselves, and you prevent others from having a chance to believe it."

The Pharisees and legal experts were furious; and from that time on they plied him fiercely with a host of questions, trying to trap him into saying something for which they could have him arrested.

Luke 11: 1–13; 27–54.

10 Love

"He Knows the Number of Hairs on Your Head!"

Meanwhile the crowds grew until thousands upon thousands were milling about and crushing each other. He turned now to his disciples and warned them, "More than anything else, beware of these Pharisees and the way they pretend to be good when they aren't. But such hypocrisy cannot be hidden forever. It will become as evident as yeast in dough. Whatever they have said in the dark shall be heard in the light, and what you have whispered in the inner rooms shall be broadcast from the housetops for all to hear!

"Dear friends, don't be afraid of these who want to murder you. They can only kill the body; they have no power over your souls. But I'll tell you whom to fear—fear God who has the power to kill and then cast into hell. What is the price of five sparrows? A couple of pennies? Not much more than that. Yet God does not forget a single one of them. And he knows the number of hairs on your head! Never fear, you are far more valuable to him than a whole flock of sparrows.

"And I assure you of this: I, the Messiah, will publicly honor you in the presence of God's angels if you publicly acknowledge me here on earth as your Friend. But I will deny before the angels those who deny me here among men. (Yet those who speak against me may be forgiven—while those who speak against the Holy Spirit shall never be forgiven.) And when you are brought to trial before these Jewish rulers and authorities in the synagogues, don't be concerned about what to say in your defense, for the Holy Spirit will give you the right words even as you are standing there."

Consider the Lilies

Then someone called from the crowd, "Sir, please tell my brother to divide my father's estate with me."

But Jesus replied, "Man, who made me a judge over you to decide such things as that? Beware! Don't always be wishing for what you don't have. For real life and real living are not related to how rich we are."

Then he gave an illustration: "A rich man had a fertile farm that produced fine crops. In fact, his barns were full to over-flowing—he couldn't get everything in. He thought about his problem, and finally exclaimed, 'I know—I'll tear down my barns and build bigger ones! Then I'll have room enough. And I'll sit back and say to myself, "Friend, you have enough stored away for years to come. Now take it easy! Wine, women, and song for you!" ' But God said to him, 'Fool! Tonight you die. Then who will get it all?' Yes, every man is a fool who gets rich on earth but not in heaven."

Then turning to his disciples he said, "Don't worry about whether you have enough food to eat or clothes to wear. For life consists of far more than food and clothes. Look at the ravens —they don't plant or harvest or have barns to store away their food, and yet they get along all right—for God feeds them. And you are far more valuable to him than any birds!

"And, besides, what's the use of worrying? What good does it do? Will it add a single day to your life? Of course not! And if worry can't even do such little things as that, what's the use of worrying over bigger things?

Luke 12: 1–26.

Consider the Lilies

"Look at the lilies! They don't toil and spin, and yet Solomon in all his glory was not robed as well as they are. And if God provides clothing for the flowers that are here today and gone tomorrow, don't you suppose that he will provide clothing for you, you doubters? And don't worry about food—what to eat and drink; don't worry at all that God will provide it for you. All mankind scratches for its daily bread, but your heavenly Father knows your needs. He will always give you all you need from day to day if you will make the Kingdom of God your primary concern.

"So don't be afraid, little flock. For it gives your Father great happiness to give you the Kingdom. Sell what you have and give to those in need. This will fatten your purses in heaven! And the purses of heaven have no rips or holes in them. Your treasures there will never disappear; no thief can steal them; no moth can destroy them. Wherever your treasure is, there your heart and thoughts will also be.

"Be prepared—all dressed and ready—for your Lord's return from the wedding feast. Then you will be ready to open the door and let him in the moment he arrives and knocks. There will be great joy for those who are ready and waiting for his return. He himself will seat them and put on a waiter's uniform and serve them as they sit and eat! He may come at nine o'clock at night—or even at midnight. But whenever he comes there will be joy for his servants who are ready! Everyone would be ready for him if they knew the exact hour of his return—just as they would be ready for a thief if they knew when he was coming. So be ready all the time. For I, the Messiah, will come when least expected."

Luke 12: 27–40.

Peter asked, "Lord are you talking just to us or to everyone?"

And the Lord replied, "I'm talking to any faithful, sensible man whose master gives him the responsibility of feeding the other servants. If his master returns and finds that he has done a good job, there will be a reward—his master will put him in charge of all he owns. But if the man begins to think, 'My Lord won't be back for a long time,' and begins to whip the men and women he is supposed to protect, and to spend his time at drinking parties and in drunkenness—well, his master will return without notice and remove him from his position of trust and assign him to the place of the unfaithful. He will be severely punished, for though he knew his duty he refused to do it. But anyone who is not aware that he is doing wrong will be punished only lightly. Much is required from those to whom much is given, for their responsibility is greater.

"I have come to bring fire to the earth, and, oh, that my task were completed! There is a terrible baptism ahead of me, and how I am pent up until it is accomplished! Do you think I have come to give peace to the earth? *No!* Rather, strife and division! From now on families will be split apart, three in favor of me, and two against—or perhaps the other way around. A father will decide one way about me; his son, the other; mother and daughter will disagree; and the decision of a mother-in-law will be spurned by her daughter-in-law."

Then he turned to the crowd and said, "When you see clouds beginning to form in the west, you say, 'Here comes a shower.' And you are right. When the south wind blows you say, 'Today will be a scorcher.' And it is. Hypocrites! You interpret the sky well enough, but you refuse to notice the warnings all around you about the crisis ahead. Why do you refuse to see for yourselves what is right? If you meet your accuser on the way to court, try to settle the matter before it reaches the judge, lest he sentence you to jail; for if that happens you won't be free again until the last penny is paid in full."

About this time he was informed that Pilate had butchered some Jews from Galilee as they were sacrificing at the Temple in Jerusalem. "Do you think they were worse sinners than other men from Galilee?" he asked. "Is that why they suffered? Not at all! And don't you realize that you also will perish unless you leave your evil ways and turn to God?

"And what about the eighteen men who died when the Tower of Siloam fell on them? Were they the worst sinners in Jerusalem? Not at all! And you, too, will perish unless you repent."

Then he used this illustration: "A man planted a fig tree in his garden and came again and again to see if he could find any fruit on it, but he was always disappointed. Finally he told his gardener to cut it down. 'I've waited three years and there hasn't been a single fig!' he said. 'Why bother with it any

longer? It's taking up space we can use for something else.'
'Give it one more chance,' the gardener answered. 'Leave it
another year, and I'll give it special attention and plenty of
fertilizer. If we get figs next year, fine; if not, I'll cut it down.' "

Luke 12: 41–59; 13: 1–9.

Crippled Woman Healed

One Sabbath as he was teaching in a synagogue, Jesus saw
a seriously handicapped woman who had been bent double for
eighteen years and was unable to straighten herself. He said,
"Woman, you are healed of your sickness!" He touched her,
and instantly she could stand straight.

But the local Jewish leader in charge of the synagogue was
very angry about it because Jesus had healed her on the Sabbath
day. "There are six days of the week to work," he shouted to
the crowd. "Those are the days to come for healing, not on the
Sabbath!"

The Lord replied, "You hypocrite! You work on the Sabbath!
Don't you untie your cattle from their stalls on the Sabbath and
lead them out for water? And is it wrong for me, just because
it is the Sabbath day, to free this Jewish woman from the
bondage in which Satan has held her for eighteen years?"

This shamed his enemies. And all the people rejoiced at the
wonderful things he did.

Now he began teaching them again about the Kingdom of
God: "What is the Kingdom like?" he asked. "How can I illustrate it? It is like a tiny mustard seed planted in a garden; soon
it grows into a tall bush, and the birds live among its branches.
It is like yeast kneaded into dough, which works unseen until
it has risen high and light."

Luke 13: 10–21.

"O Jerusalem, Jerusalem!"

Jesus went from city to city and village to village, teaching as
he went, always pressing onward toward Jerusalem. Someone
asked him, "Will only a few be saved?"

"O Jerusalem, Jerusalem!"

And he replied, "The door to heaven is narrow. Work hard to get in, for the truth is that many will try to enter but when the head of the house has locked the door, it will be too late. Then if you stand outside knocking, and pleading, 'Lord, open the door for us,' he will reply, 'I do not know you.' But we ate with you, and you taught in our streets,' you will say. And he will reply, 'I tell you, I don't know you. You can't come in here, guilty as you are. Go away.' And there will be great weeping and gnashing of teeth as you stand outside and see Abraham, Isaac, Jacob and all the prophets within the Kingdom of God— for people will come from all over the world to take their places there. And note this: some who are despised now will be greatly honored then; and some who are highly thought of now will be least important then."

A few minutes later some Pharisees said to him, "Get out of here if you want to live, for King Herod is after you!" Jesus replied, "Go tell that fox that I will keep on casting out demons and doing miracles of healing today and tomorrow; and the third day I will reach my destination. Yes, today, tomorrow, and the next day! For it wouldn't do for a prophet of God to be killed except in Jerusalem!

"O Jerusalem, Jerusalem! The city that murders the prophets. The city stones those sent to help her. How often I have wanted to gather your children together even as a hen protects her brood under her wings, but you wouldn't let me. And now— now your house is left desolate. And you will never again see me until you say, 'Welcome to him who comes in the name of the Lord.' "

As Jesus and the disciples continued on their way to Jerusalem they came to a village where a woman named Martha welcomed them into her home. Her sister Mary sat on the floor, listening to Jesus as he talked. But Martha was the jittery type, and was worrying over the big dinner she was preparing. She came to Jesus and said, "Sir, doesn't it seem unfair to you that my sister just sits here while I do all the work? Tell her to come and help me."

But the Lord said to her, "Martha, dear friend, you are so

upset over all these details! There is really only one thing worth being concerned about. Mary has discovered it—and I won't take it away from her!"

Once again the Jews started to arrest him. But he went beyond the Jordan River to stay near the place where John was first baptizing.

Luke 13: 22–35; 10: 38–42; John 10: 39–40.

One Sabbath as Jesus was in the home of a member of the Jewish Council, the Pharisees were watching him like hawks to see if he would heal a man who was present who was suffering from dropsy. He said to the Pharisees and legal experts standing around, "Well, is it within the Law to heal a man on the Sabbath day, or not?" And when they refused to answer, Jesus took the sick man by the hand and healed him and sent him away. Then he turned to them: "Which of you doesn't work on the Sabbath?" he asked. "If your cow falls into a pit, don't you proceed at once to get it out?" Again they had no answer.

When he noticed that all who came to the dinner were trying to sit near the head of the table, he gave them this advice: "If you are invited to a wedding feast, don't always head for the best seat. For if someone more respected than you shows up, the host will bring him over to where you are sitting and say, 'Let this man sit here instead.' And you, embarrassed, will have to take whatever seat is left at the foot of the table! Do this instead —start at the foot; and when your host sees you he will come and say, 'Friend, we have a better place than this for you!' Thus you will be honored in front of all the other guests. For everyone who tries to honor himself shall be humbled; and he who humbles himself shall be honored." Then he turned to his host.

Luke 14: 1–12.

Everybody May Come

"When you put on a dinner," he said, "don't invite friends, brothers, relatives and rich neighbors! For they will return the invitation. Instead, invite the poor, the crippled, the lame, and the blind. Then at the resurrection of the godly, God will reward you for inviting those who can't repay you."

A man sitting at the table with Jesus exclaimed, "What a privilege it would be to get into the Kingdom of God!"

Jesus replied with this illustration: "A man prepared a great feast and sent out many invitations. When all was ready, he sent his servant around to notify the guests that it was time for them to arrive. But they all began making excuses. One said he had just bought a field and wanted to inspect it, and asked to be excused. Another said he had just bought five pair of oxen and wanted to try them out. Another had just been married and for that reason couldn't come.

"The servant returned and reported to his master what they had said. His master was angry and told him to go quickly into the streets and alleys of the city and to invite the beggars, crippled, lame, and blind. But even then, there was still room. 'Well then,' said his master, 'go out into the country lanes and out behind the hedges and urge anyone you find to come, so that the house will be full. For none of those I invited first will get even the smallest taste of what I had prepared for them.' "

Great crowds were following him. He turned around and addressed them as follows: "Anyone who wants to be my follower must love me far more than he does his own father, mother, wife, children, brothers, or sisters—yes, more than his own life—otherwise he cannot be my disciple. And no one can be my disciple who does not carry his own cross and follow me.

"But don't begin until you count the cost. For who would begin construction of a building without first getting estimates and then checking to see if he has enough money to pay the bills? Otherwise he might complete only the foundation before running out of funds. And then how everyone would laugh! 'See that fellow there?' they would mock. 'He started that building and ran out of money before it was finished!'

"Or what king would ever dream of going to war without first sitting down with his counselors and discussing whether his army of 10,000 is strong enough to defeat the 20,000 men who are marching against him? If the decision is negative, then while the enemy troops are still far away, he will send a truce team to discuss terms of peace.

"So no one can become my disciple unless he first sits down and counts his blessings—and then renounces them all for me. What good is salt that has lost its saltiness? Flavorless salt is fit for nothing—not even for fertilizer. It is worthless and must be thrown out. Listen well, if you would understand my meaning."

Luke 14: 12–35.

The Ninety and Nine

Dishonest tax collectors and other notorious sinners often came to listen to Jesus' sermons; but this caused complaints from the Jewish religious leaders and the experts on Jewish law because he was associating with such despicable people—even eating with them!

So Jesus used this illustration: "If you had a hundred sheep and one of them strayed away and was lost in the wilderness, wouldn't you leave the ninety-nine others to go and search for the lost one until you found it? And then you would joyfully carry it home on your shoulders. When you arrived you would call together your friends and neighbors to rejoice with you because your lost sheep was found. Well, in the same way heaven will be happier over one lost sinner who returns to God than over ninety-nine others who haven't strayed away!

"Or take another illustration: A woman has ten valuable silver coins and loses one. Won't she light a lamp and look in every corner of the house and sweep every nook and cranny until she finds it? And then won't she call in her friends and neighbors to rejoice with her? In the same way there is joy in the presence of the angels of God when one sinner repents."

To further illustrate the point, he told them this story: "A man had two sons. When the younger told his father, 'I want my share of your estate now, instead of waiting until you die!' his father agreed to divide his wealth between his sons. A few

The Prodigal Welcomed Home

days later this younger son packed all his belongings and took a trip to a distant land, and there wasted all his money on parties and prostitutes. About the time his money was gone a great famine swept over the land, and he began to starve. He persuaded a local farmer to hire him to feed his pigs. The boy became so hungry that even the pods he was feeding the swine looked good to him. And no one gave him anything.

"When he finally came to his senses, he said to himself, 'At home even the hired men have food enough and to spare, and here I am, dying of hunger! I will go home to my father and say, "Father, I have sinned against both heaven and you, and am no longer worthy of being called your son. Please take me on as a hired man." ' So he returned home to his father. And while he was still a long distance away, his father saw him coming, and was filled with loving pity and ran and embraced him and kissed him.

Luke 15: 1–20.

The Prodigal Welcomed Home

"His son said to him, 'Father, I have sinned against heaven and you, and am not worthy of being called your son—' But his father said to the slaves, 'Quick! Bring the finest robe in the house and put it on him. And a jeweled ring for his finger; and shoes! And kill the calf we have in the fattening pen. We must celebrate with a feast, for this son of mine was dead and has returned to life. He was lost and is found.' So the party began.

"Meanwhile, the older son was in the fields working; when he returned home, he heard dance music coming from the house, and he asked one of the servants what was going on. 'Your brother is back,' he was told, 'and your father has killed the calf we were fattening and has prepared a great feast to celebrate his coming home again unharmed.'

"The older brother was angry and wouldn't go in. His father came out and begged him, but he replied, 'All these years I've worked hard for you and never once refused to do a single thing you told me to; and in all that time you never gave me even one young goat for a feast with my friends. Yet when this son of yours comes back after spending your money on prostitutes, you celebrate by killing the finest calf we have on the place.'

" 'Look, dear son,' his father said to him, 'you and I are very close, and everything I have is yours. But it is right to celebrate. For he is your brother; and he was dead and has come back to life! He was lost and is found!' "

Luke 15: 21–32.

"You Cannot Serve Both God and Money"

Jesus now told this story to his disciples: "A rich man hired an accountant to handle his affairs, but soon a rumor went around that the accountant was thoroughly dishonest. So his employer called him in and said, 'What's this I hear about your stealing from me? Get your report in order, for you are to be dismissed.'

"The accountant thought to himself, 'Now what? I'm through here, and I haven't the strength to go out and dig ditches, and I'm too proud to beg. I know just the thing! And then I'll have plenty of friends to take care of me when I leave!' So he invited each one who owed money to his employer to come and discuss the situation. He asked the first one, 'How much do you owe him?' 'My debt is 850 gallons of olive oil,' the man replied. 'Yes, here is the contract you signed,' the accountant told him. 'Tear it up and write another one for half that much!' 'And how much do you owe him?' he asked the next man. 'A thousand bushels of wheat,' was the reply. 'Here,' the accountant said, 'take your note and replace it with one for only 800 bushels!'

"The rich man had to admire the rascal for being so shrewd. And it is true that the citizens of this world are more clever in dishonesty than the godly are. But shall I tell *you* to act that way, to buy friendship through cheating? Will this ensure your entry into an everlasting home in heaven? *No!* For unless you are honest in small matters, you won't be in large ones. If you cheat even a little, you won't be honest with greater responsibilities. And if you are untrustworthy about worldly wealth, who will trust you with the true riches of heaven? And if you are not faithful with other people's money, why should you be entrusted with money of your own?

"For neither you nor anyone else can serve two masters. You will hate one and show loyalty to the other, or else the other way around—you will be enthusiastic about one and despise the other. You cannot serve both God and money."

The Pharisees, who dearly loved their money, naturally scoffed at all this. Then he said to them, "You wear a noble, pious expression in public, but God knows your evil hearts. Your pretense brings you honor from the people, but it is an abomination in the sight of God.

"Until John the Baptist began to preach, the laws of Moses and the messages of the prophets were your guides. But John introduced the Good News that the Kingdom of God would come soon. And now eager multitudes are pressing in. But that doesn't mean that the Law has lost its force in even the smallest point. It is as strong and unshakable as heaven and earth. So anyone who divorces his wife and marries someone else commits adultery, and anyone who marries a divorced woman commits adultery.

"There was a certain rich man," Jesus said, "who was splendidly clothed and lived each day in mirth and luxury. One day Lazarus, a diseased beggar, was laid at his door. As he lay there longing for scraps from the rich man's table, the dogs would come and lick his open sores. Finally the beggar died and was carried by the angels to be with Abraham in the place of the righteous dead. The rich man also died and was buried, and his soul went into hell. There, in torment, he saw Lazarus in the far distance with Abraham. 'Father Abraham,' he shouted, 'have some pity! Send Lazarus over here if only to dip the tip of his finger in water and cool my tongue, for I am in anguish in these flames.' But Abraham said to him, 'Son, remember that during your lifetime you had everything you wanted, and Lazarus had nothing. So now he is here being comforted and you are in anguish. And besides, there is a great chasm separating us, and anyone wanting to come to you from here is stopped at its edge; and no one over there can cross to us.'

"Then the rich man said, 'O Father Abraham, then please send him to my father's home—for I have five brothers—to warn them about this place of torment lest they come here when they die.' But Abraham said, 'The Scriptures have warned them again and again. Your brothers can read them any time they want to.' The rich man replied, 'No, Father Abraham, they won't bother to read them. But if someone is sent to them from the dead, then they will turn from their sins.' But Abraham said, 'If they won't listen to Moses and the prophets, they won't listen even though someone rises from the dead.' "

Luke 16: 1–31.

"There will always be temptations to sin," Jesus said one day to his disciples, "but woe to the man who does the tempting. If he were thrown into the sea with a huge rock tied to his neck, he would be far better off than facing the punishment in store for those who harm these little children's souls. I am warning you! Rebuke your brother if he sins, and forgive him if he is sorry. Even if he wrongs you seven times a day and each time turns again and asks forgiveness, forgive him."

One day the apostles said to the Lord, "We need more faith; tell us how to get it."

"If your faith were only the size of a mustard seed," Jesus answered, "it would be large enough to uproot that mulberry tree over there and send it hurtling into the sea! Your command would bring immediate results! When a servant comes in from plowing or taking care of sheep, he doesn't just sit down and eat, but first prepares his master's meal and serves him his supper before he eats his own. And he is not even thanked, for he is merely doing what he is supposed to do. Just so, if you merely obey me, you should not consider yourselves worthy of praise. For you have simply done your duty!"

Luke 17: 1–10.

Lazarus Raised from the Dead

Lazarus, who lived in Bethany, the brother of Mary and Martha, was sick. You remember Mary, who poured the costly perfume on Jesus' feet and wiped them with her hair? The sisters sent a message to Jesus telling him, "Sir, your good friend is very, very sick."

Jesus said, "The purpose of his illness is not death, but for the glory of God. I, the Son of God, will receive glory from this situation."

Although Jesus was very fond of Martha, Mary, and Lazarus, he stayed where he was for the next two days. Finally, he said to his disciples, "Let's go to Judea."

His disciples objected. "Master," they said, "only a few days ago the Jewish leaders in Judea were trying to kill you. Are you going there again?"

Jesus replied, "There are twelve hours of daylight every day, and during every hour of it a man can walk safely and not stumble. Only at night is there danger of a wrong step, because of the dark. Our friend Lazarus has gone to sleep, but now I will go and waken him!"

The disciples, thinking Jesus meant Lazarus was having a good night's rest, said, "That means he is getting better!" But Jesus meant Lazarus had died.

Then he told them plainly, "Lazarus is dead. And for your sake, I am glad I wasn't there, for this will give you another opportunity to believe in me. Come, let's go to him."

When they arrived at Bethany, they were told that Lazarus had already been in his tomb for four days. When Martha got word that Jesus was coming, she went to meet him. But Mary stayed at home. Martha said to Jesus, "Sir, if you had been here, my brother wouldn't have died. And even now it's not too late, for I know that God will bring my brother back to life again, if you will only ask him to."

Jesus told her, "Your brother will come back to life again."

"Yes," Martha said, "when everyone else does, on Resurrection Day."

Jesus told her, "I am the one who raises the dead and gives them life again. Anyone who believes in me, even though he dies like anyone else, shall live again. He is given eternal life for believing in me and shall never perish. Do you believe this, Martha?"

"Yes, Master," she told him. "I believe you are the Messiah, the Son of God, the one we have so long awaited."

Then she left him and returned to Mary and calling her aside from the mourners, told her, "Jesus is here." Mary went to him at once. The Jewish leaders who were at the house trying to console Mary followed her.

Mary fell down at Jesus' feet, saying, "Sir, if you had been here, my brother would still be alive."

Jesus saw her weeping; he was moved with indignation and deeply troubled. "Where is he buried?" he asked them.

They told him, "Come and see." Tears came to Jesus' eyes. "They were close friends," the Jewish leaders said. "See how much he loved him."

Jesus came to the tomb. It was a cave with a heavy stone rolled across its door. "Roll the stone aside," Jesus told them.

Martha, the dead man's sister, said, "He has been dead four days."

"But didn't I tell you that you will see a wonderful miracle from God if you believe?" Jesus asked her. So they rolled the stone aside. Then Jesus looked up to heaven and said, "Father, thank you for hearing me. (You always hear me, of course, but I said it because of all these people standing here, so that they will believe you sent me.)" Then he shouted, "Lazarus, come out!" Lazarus came—bound up in the gravecloth. Jesus told them, "Unwrap him and let him go!"

Then the chief priests and Pharisees convened a council to discuss the situation. "What are we going to do!" they asked each other. "For this man certainly does miracles. If we let him alone the whole nation will follow him—and then the Roman army will come and kill us and take over the Jewish government." So from that time on the Jewish leaders began plotting Jesus death.

Jesus now stopped his public ministry and left Jerusalem; he went to the edge of the desert, to the village of Ephraim, and stayed there with his disciples.

John 11: 1–54.

"Your Faith Has Made You Well"

As they continued toward Jerusalem, they reached Galilee and Samaria, and as they entered a village there, ten lepers stood at a distance, crying out, "Jesus, sir, have mercy on us!"

He said, "Go to the Jewish priest and show him that you are healed!" As they were going, their leprosy disappeared.

One of them came back to Jesus. He fell flat on the ground in front of Jesus, thanking him for what he had done. This man was a despised Samaritan. Jesus asked, "Didn't I heal ten men? Where are the nine? Does only this foreigner return to give glory to God?" And Jesus said to the man, "Stand up and go; your faith has made you well."

One day the Pharisees asked Jesus, "When will the Kingdom of God begin?"

Jesus replied, "The Kingdom of God isn't ushered in with visible signs. You won't be able to say, 'It has begun here in this place or there in that part of the country.' For the Kingdom of God is within you."

Later he talked again about this with his disciples. "The time is coming when you will long for me to be with you even for a single day, but I won't be here," he said. Reports will reach you that I have returned and that I am in this place or that; don't believe it or go out to look for me. For when I return, you will know it beyond all doubt. It will be as evident as the lightning that flashes across the skies. But first I must suffer terribly and be rejected by this whole nation.

"When I return the world will be as indifferent to the things of God as the people were in Noah's day. They ate and drank and married—everything just as usual right up to the day when Noah went into the ark and the flood came and destroyed them all. And the world will be as it was in the days of Lot; people went about their daily business—eating and drinking, buying and selling, farming and building—until the morning Lot left Sodom. Then fire and brimstone rained down from heaven and destroyed them all. Yes, it will be 'business as usual' right up to the hour of my return.

"Those away from home that day must not return to pack; those in the fields must not return to town—remember what happened to Lot's wife! Whoever clings to his life shall lose it, and whoever loses his life shall save it. That night two men will be asleep in the same room, and one will be taken away, the other left. Two women will be working together at household tasks; one will be taken, the other left; and so it will be with men working side by side in the fields."

"Lord, where will they be taken?" the disciples asked.

Jesus replied, "Where the body is, the vultures gather!"

Jesus told his disciples a story to illustrate their need for constant prayer and to show them that they must keep praying until the answer comes. "There was a city judge," he said, "a very godless man who had great contempt for everyone. A widow of that city came to him frequently to appeal for justice against a man who had harmed her. The judge ignored her for a while, but eventually she got on his nerves. 'I fear neither God nor man,' he said to himself, 'but this woman bothers me. I'm going to see that she gets justice, for she is wearing me out with her constant coming!' "

Then the Lord said, "If even an evil judge can be worn down like that, don't you think that God will surely give justice to his people who plead with him day and night? Yes! He will answer them quickly! But the question is: When I, the Messiah, return, how many will I find who have faith and are praying?"

Luke 17: 11–37; 18: 1–8.

He Loved Little Children

Jesus told this story to some who boasted of their virtue and scorned everyone else: "Two men went to the Temple to pray. One was a proud, self-righteous Pharisee, and the other a cheating tax collector.

"The proud Pharisee 'prayed' this prayer: 'Thank God, I am not a sinner like everyone else, especially like that tax collector over there! For I never cheat, I don't commit adultery, I go without food twice a week, and I give to God a tenth of everything I earn.' But the corrupt tax collector stood at a distance and dared not even lift his eyes to heaven as he prayed, but beat upon his chest in sorrow, exclaiming, 'God, be merciful to me, a sinner.'

"I tell you, this sinner, not the Pharisee, returned home forgiven! For the proud shall be humbled, but the humble shall be honored."

Luke 18: 9–14; Mark 10: 13–14.

He Loved Little Children

Once when some mothers were bringing their children to Jesus to bless them, the disciples shooed them away, telling them not to bother him. But when Jesus saw what was happening he was very much displeased with his disciples and said to them, "Let the little children come to me, and don't prevent them. For of such is the Kingdom of Heaven. I tell you as seriously as I know how that anyone who refuses to come to God as a little child will never be allowed into his Kingdom." Then he took the children into his arms and placed his hands on their heads and he blessed them before he left.

As he was starting out on a trip a Jewish religious leader came running and knelt down and asked, "Good Teacher, what must I do to have eternal life?"

"Do you realize what you are saying when you call me 'good'?" Jesus asked him. "Only God is truly good, and no one else. But to answer your question, you can get to heaven if you keep the commandments."

"Which ones?" the man asked.

"You know the commandments: don't kill, don't commit

adultery, don't steal, don't lie, don't cheat, respect your father and mother, and love your neighbor as yourself!"

"I've always obeyed every one of them," the youth replied. "What else must I do?"

Jesus felt genuine love for this man as he looked at him. "You lack only one thing," he told him. "If you want to be perfect, go and sell everything you have and give the money to the poor, and you will have treasure in heaven; and come, follow me." But when the young man heard this, he went away sadly, for he was very rich.

Jesus turned around and said, "How hard it is for the rich to enter the Kingdom of God! It is easier for a camel to go through the eye of a needle than for a rich man to enter the Kingdom of God." This amazed them.

So Jesus said it again: "Dear children, how hard it is for those who trust in riches to enter the Kingdom of God. It is almost impossible for a rich man to get into the Kingdom of Heaven. I say it again—it is easier for a camel to go through the eye of a needle than for a rich man to enter the Kingdom of God!" This remark confounded the disciples. "Then who in the world can be saved?" they asked.

Jesus said, "Without God, it is utterly impossible. But with God everything is possible."

Then Peter said to him, "We left everything to follow you. What will we get out of it?"

And Jesus replied, "When I, the Messiah, shall sit upon my glorious throne in the Kingdom, you my disciples shall certainly sit on twelve thrones judging the twelve tribes of Israel. Anyone who gives up his home, brothers, sisters, father, mother, wife, children, or property for the sake of the Kingdom of God, for love of me and to tell others the Good News, shall receive a hundred times as much in return, and shall have eternal life. Let me assure you that no one has ever given up anything—home, brothers, sisters, mother, father, children or property—for love of me and to tell others the Good News, who won't be given back, a hundred times over, homes, brothers, sisters, mothers, children, and land—with persecutions, as well as receiving eternal life in the world to come. But many who are first now will be last then; and some who are last now will be first then."

Here is another illustration of the Kingdom of Heaven. "The owner of an estate went out early one morning to hire workers for his harvest field. He agreed to pay them $20 a day* and sent them out to work. A couple of hours later he was passing a hiring hall and saw some men standing around waiting for jobs, so he sent them also into his fields, telling them he would pay them whatever was right at the end of the day. At noon and again around three o'clock in the afternoon he did the same thing. At five o'clock that evening he was in town again and saw some more men standing around and asked them, 'Why haven't you been working today?' 'Because no one hired us,' they replied. 'Then go on out and join the others in my fields,' he told them.

"That evening he told the paymaster to call the men in and pay them, beginning with the last men first. When the men hired at five o'clock were paid, each received $20. So when the men hired earlier came to get theirs, they assumed they would receive much more. But they, too, were paid $20. They protested, 'Those fellows worked only one hour, and yet you've paid them just as much as those of us who worked all day in the scorching heat.' 'Friend,' he answered one of them, 'I did you no wrong! Didn't you agree to work all day for $20? Take it and go. It is my desire to pay all the same; is it against the law to give away my money if I want to? Should you be angry because I am kind?' And so it is that the last shall be first, and the first, last."

Matthew 19: 13–30; 20: 1–16; Mark 10: 13–30; Luke 18: 19–30.

Huge Crowds Follow Him

Southward to the Judean borders into the area east of the Jordan River, vast crowds followed him, and as usual he taught them. Some Pharisees came and tried to trap him asking, "Do you permit divorce?"

*Literally, "a denarius," the payment for a day's labor; equivalent to $20 in modern times.

"What did Moses say about divorce?" Jesus asked them.

"He said it was all right," they replied. "He said that all a man has to do is write his wife a letter of dismissal."

"And why did he say that?" Jesus asked. "I'll tell you why —it was a concession to your hardhearted wickedness. But it certainly isn't God's way. For from the very first he made man and woman to be joined together permanently in marriage; therefore a man is to leave his father and mother. Don't you read the Scriptures? In them it is written that at the beginning God created man and woman, and that a man should leave his father and mother, and be forever united to his wife. The two shall become one—no longer two, but one! And no man may divorce what God has joined together."

"Then, why," they asked, "did Moses say a man may divorce his wife by merely writing her a letter of dismissal?" Jesus replied, "Moses did that in recognition of your hard and evil hearts, but it was not what God had originally intended. And I tell you this, that anyone who divorces his wife, except for fornication, and marries another, commits adultery.

Later, in the house, his disciples brought up the subject again. He told them, "When a man divorces his wife to marry someone else, he commits adultery against her. And if a wife divorces her husband and remarries, she, too, commits adultery."

Jesus' disciples then said to him, "If that is how it is, it is better not to marry!"

"Not everyone can accept this statement," Jesus said. "Only those whom God helps. Some are born without the ability to marry, and some are disabled by men, and some refuse to marry for the sake of the Kingdom of Heaven. Let anyone who can, accept my statement."

Mark 10: 1–12; Matthew 19: 1–12.

11 Servant

"The Greatest of All Must Be the Servant of All"

Jesus, on the way to Jerusalem, again took the disciples aside and began describing all that was going to happen to him when they arrived at Jerusalem.

"When we get there," he told them, "I, the Messiah, will be betrayed and arrested and taken before the chief priests and the Jewish leaders, and treated shamefully and spat upon and sentenced to die. They will hand me over to the Roman government. They will mock me and flog me with their whips and crucify and kill me; but after three days I will come back to life again. All the predictions of the ancient prophets concerning me will come true."

But they didn't understand a thing he said. He seemed to be talking in riddles.

Then the mother of James and John, the sons of Zebedee, respectfully asked a favor. "What is your request?" he asked. She replied, "In your Kingdom, will you let my two sons sit on two thrones next to yours?" But Jesus told her, "You don't know what you are asking!" Then he turned to James and John and asked them, "Are you able to drink from the terrible cup I am about to drink from?" "Yes," they replied, "we are able." And Jesus said, "You shall indeed drink from my cup and be baptized with my baptism, but I do not have the right to place you on thrones next to mine. Those places are reserved for the persons my Father selects."

The other ten disciples were indignant when they heard what James and John had asked for. But Jesus called them together

and said, "Among the heathen, kings are tyrants and each mi-
nor official lords it over those beneath him. The kings and great
men of the earth lord it over the people; but among you it is
different. Whoever wants to be great among you must be your
servant. And whoever wants to be greatest of all must be the
slave of all. For even I, the Messiah, am not here to be served,
but to help others, and to give my life as a ransom for many."

Matthew 20: 17-25; Mark 10: 32-45; Luke 18: 31-34.

The Blind Healed

A crowd followed Jesus. As they approached Jericho, a blind
man was sitting beside the road, begging. When he heard the
noise of a crowd, he asked what was happening. He was told
that Jesus from Nazareth was going by, so he began shouting,
"Jesus, Son of David, have mercy on me!"

"Bring the blind man over here," Jesus said. Jesus asked the
man, "What do you want?"

"Lord," he pleaded, "I want to see!"

And Jesus said, "All right, begin seeing! Your faith has healed
you." Instantly the man could see.

And so they reached Jericho. Later, as they left town, a blind
beggar named Bartimaeus was sitting beside the road. When
Bartimaeus heard that Jesus from Nazareth was near, he began
to shout out, "Jesus, Son of David, have mercy on me!"

"Shut up!" some of the people yelled at him.

But he only shouted the louder, again and again, "O Son of
David, have mercy on me!"

Jesus said, "Tell him to come here." They called the blind
man.

"You lucky fellow," they said, "come on, he's calling you!"
Bartimaeus yanked off his old coat and came to Jesus.

"What do you want me to do for you?" Jesus asked.

"O Teacher," the blind man said, "I want to see!"

And Jesus said to him, "All right, it's done. Your faith has
healed you." And instantly the blind man could see, and followed Jesus down the road!

As Jesus was passing through Jericho, a man named Zacch-

The Blind Healed

aeus, one of the most influential Jews in the Roman tax-collecting business (a very rich man), tried to get a look at Jesus, but he was too short to see over the crowds. So he ran ahead and climbed into a sycamore tree to watch from there. When Jesus came by he looked up at Zacchaeus and called, "Zacchaeus! Quick! Come down! For I am going to be a guest in your home today!"

Zacchaeus climbed down and took Jesus to his house in great excitement and joy. But the crowds were displeased. "He has gone to be the guest of a notorious sinner," they grumbled.

Zacchaeus stood before the Lord and said, "Sir, from now on I will give half my wealth to the poor, and if I find I have overcharged anyone on his taxes, I will penalize myself by giving him back four times as much!"

Jesus told him, "This shows that salvation has come to this home today. This man was one of the lost sons of Abraham, and I, the Messiah, have come to search for and to save such souls as his."

And because Jesus was nearing Jerusalem, he told a story to correct the impression that the Kingdom of God would begin right away. "A nobleman living in a certain province was called away to the distant capital of the empire to be crowned king of his province. Before he left he called together ten assistants and gave them each $2,000 to invest while he was gone. But some of his people hated him and sent him their declaration of independence, stating that they had rebelled and would not acknowledge him as their king."

Upon his return he called in the men to whom he had given the money, to find out what they had done with it, and what their profits were. The first man reported a tremendous gain—ten times as much as the original amount! 'Fine!' the king exclaimed. 'You are a good man. You have been faithful with the little I entrusted to you, and as your reward, you shall be governor of ten cities.' The next man also reported a splendid gain—five times the original amount. 'All right!' his master said. 'You can be governor over five cities.'

"But the third man brought back only the money he had

started with. 'I've kept it safe,' he said, 'because I was afraid you would demand my profits, for you are a hard man to deal with, taking what isn't yours and even confiscating the crops that others plant.' 'You vile and wicked slave,' the king roared. 'Hard, am I? That's exactly how I'll be toward you! If you knew so much about me and how tough I am, then why didn't you deposit the money in the bank so that I could at least get some interest on it?' Then turning to the others standing by he ordered, 'Take the money away from him and give it to the man who earned the most. 'But, sir,' they said, 'he has enough already!'

'And now about these enemies of mine who revolted—bring them in and execute them before me. It is always true that those who have, get more, and those who have little, soon lose even that.' "

Luke 18: 35–43; 19: 1–27; Mark 10: 46–52.

"Long Live the King!"

The Passover, a Jewish holy day, was near, and many country people arrived in Jerusalem several days early so that they could go through the cleansing ceremony before the Passover began.

Jesus went on towards Jerusalem, walking along ahead of his disciples. Meanwhile the chief priests and Pharisees had publicly announced that anyone seeing Jesus must report him immediately so that they could arrest him.

As Jesus came to the towns of Bethphage and Bethany, on the Mount of Olives, he sent two disciples ahead. "Go into that village over there," he told them, "and just as you enter you will see a donkey tied there, with its colt beside it, that has never been ridden. Untie them and bring them here. If anyone asks you what you are doing, just say, 'The Master needs them,' and there will be no trouble."

The two disciples did as Jesus said. As they were untying it, the owners demanded an explanation. "What are you doing?" they asked. "Why are you untying our colt?" And the disciples simply replied, "The Lord needs him!" And then the men agreed.

They brought the animals to him and threw their garments over the colt for him to ride on. Many in the crowd spread out their coats along the road before him, while others threw down leafy branches.

As they reached the place where the road started down from the Mount of Olives, the whole procession praised God. "God has given us a King!" they exulted. "Long live the King! Let all heaven rejoice!"

Some of the Pharisees said, "Sir, rebuke your followers for saying things like that!"

He replied, "If they keep quiet, the stones along the road will burst into cheers!"

John 11: 55–57; Matthew 21: 2–7; Mark 11: 2–8; Luke 19: 28–40.

Jesus Weeps Over the City

But as they came closer to Jerusalem and he saw the city ahead, he began to cry. "Eternal peace was within your reach and you turned it down," he wept, "and now it is too late. Your enemies will pile up earth against your walls and encircle you and close in on you, and crush you to the ground, and your children within you; your enemies will not leave one stone upon another—for you have rejected the opportunity God offered you."

The entire city of Jerusalem was stirred as he entered. He taught daily in the temple. The blind and crippled came to him and he healed them.

These wonderful miracles, and the little children in the Temple shouting, "God bless the Son of David," disturbed the chief priests and other Jewish leaders. They asked him, "Do you hear what these children are saying?"

"Yes," Jesus replied. "Didn't you ever read the Scriptures? For they say, 'Even little babies shall praise him!' "

He looked around carefully at everything and then left—for

now it was late in the afternoon—and went out to Bethany with the twelve disciples where he stayed overnight.

Luke 19: 41–44; Matthew 21: 10–17; Mark 11: 11.

The next morning as they left Bethany returning to Jerusalem, Jesus was hungry. A little way off he noticed a fig tree in full leaf, so he went over to see if he could find any figs on it. But no, there were only leaves, for it was too early in the season for fruit. He said, "Never bear fruit again!" And soon the fig tree withered up.

The disciples were utterly amazed and asked, "How did the fig tree wither so quickly?"

Jesus told them, "Truly, if you have faith, and don't doubt, you can do things like this and much more. You can even say to this Mount of Olives, 'Move over into the ocean,' and it will. You can get anything—*anything* you ask for in prayer—if you believe."

When they arrived back to Jerusalem Jesus went to the Temple and began to drive out the merchants and their customers, and knocked over the tables of the money-changers and the stalls of those selling doves, and stopped everyone from bringing in loads of merchandise. He told them, "My Temple is a place of prayer. It is written in the Scriptures, 'My Temple is to be a place of prayer for all nations,' but you have turned it into a den of robbers."

When the chief priests and other Jewish leaders heard what he had done they began planning how best to get rid of him. But they could think of nothing, for he was a hero to the people —they hung on every word he said.

That evening they left the city. Next morning, as they passed the fig tree, they saw that it was withered from the roots! Peter remembered what Jesus had said to the tree, and exclaimed, "Look, Teacher! The fig tree you cursed has withered!"

Mark 11: 12–21; Matthew 21: 12–13; 18–22; Luke 19: 45–48.

Faith Removes Mountains

In reply Jesus said, "If you only have faith in God—this is the absolute truth—you can say to this Mount of Olives, 'Rise up and fall into the Mediterranean,' and your command will be obeyed. All that's required is that you really believe and have no doubt! Listen to me! You can pray for *anything,* and *if you believe, you have it;* it's yours! But when you are praying, first forgive anyone you are holding a grudge against, so that your Father in heaven will forgive you your sins too."*

Mark 11:22–26.

On one of those days as he was walking in the Temple and preaching the Good News, Jesus was confronted by the chief priests and other religious leaders and councilmen. They demanded to know by what authority he had driven out the merchants from the Temple. Jesus replied, "I'll tell you if you answer one question! What about John the Baptist? Was he sent by God, or not? Answer me!"

They talked it over among themselves. "If we say his message was from heaven, then he will ask, 'Then why didn't you believe him?' But if we say John was not sent from God, the people will mob us, for they are convinced that he was a prophet." Finally they replied, "We don't know!"

And Jesus responded, "Then I won't answer your question either."

Then he told these story-illustrations: "But what do you think about this? A man with two sons told the older boy, 'Son, go out and work on the farm today.' 'I won't,' he answered, but later he changed his mind and went. Then the father told the youngest, 'You go!' and he said, 'Yes, sir, I will.' But he didn't. Which of the two was obeying his father?"

They replied, "The first, of course."

Then Jesus explained his meaning: "Surely evil men and

---

*Many ancient authorities add, "but if you do not forgive, neither will your Father who is in heaven forgive your trespasses."

prostitutes will get into the Kingdom before you do. For John the Baptist told you to repent and turn to God, and you wouldn't, while very evil men and prostitutes did. And even when you saw this happening, you refused to repent, and so you couldn't believe.

"Now listen to this story: A certain landowner planted a vineyard and built a wall around it and dug a pit for pressing out the grape juice, and built a watchman's tower. Then he leased the farm to tenant farmers and moved to another country. When harvest time came, he sent one of his men to the farm to collect his share of the crops. But the tenants beat him up and sent him back empty-handed. The owner then sent another of his men, who received the same treatment, only worse, for his head was seriously injured. The next man he sent was killed. He sent a larger group but the results were the same, his men were either beaten or killed. There was only one left—his only son.

" 'What shall I do?' the owner asked himself. 'I'll send my cherished son.' He finally sent him, thinking they would surely give him their full respect. But when the farmers saw him coming they said, 'He will own the farm when his father dies. Come on, let's kill him—and then the farm will be ours!' So they caught him and murdered him and threw his body out of the vineyard.

"When the owner returns, what do you think he will do to those farmers? He will put the wicked men to a horrible death, and lease the vineyard to others who will pay him promptly."

"But they would never do a thing like that," his listeners protested.

Jesus looked at them and said, "Didn't you ever read in the Scriptures: 'The stone rejected by the builders has been made the honored cornerstone. This is the Lord's doing and it is an amazing thing to see'?

"What I mean is that the Kingdom of God shall be taken away from you, and given to a nation that will give God his share of the crop. All who stumble on this rock of truth shall be broken, but those it falls on will be scattered as dust."

When the chief priests and other Jewish leaders realized that Jesus was talking about them—that they were the farmers in his story—they wanted to get rid of him, but were afraid to try because of the crowds, for they accepted Jesus as a prophet. So they left him and went away.

Matthew 21: 28–46; Mark 11: 27–30; 12: 1–12; Luke 20: 1–17.

Caesar's and God's

Jesus told several other stories to show what the Kingdom of Heaven is like. "For instance," he said, "it can be illustrated by the story of a king who prepared a great wedding dinner for his son. Many guests were invited, and when the banquet was ready he sent messengers to notify everyone that it was time to come. But all refused! So he sent other servants to tell them, 'Everything is ready and the roast is in the oven. Hurry!' But the guests he had invited merely laughed and went on about their business, one to his farm, another to his store; others beat up his messengers and treated them shamefully, even killing some of them.

"Then the angry king sent out his army and destroyed the murderers and burned their city. And he said to his servants, 'The wedding feast is ready, and the guests I invited aren't worthy of the honor. Now go out to the street corners and invite everyone you see.' So the servants did, and brought in all they could find, good and bad alike; and the banquet hall was filled with guests.

"But when the king came in to meet the guests he noticed a man who wasn't wearing the wedding robe provided for him. 'Friend,' he asked, 'how does it happen that you are here without a wedding robe?' And the man had no reply. Then the king said to his aides, 'Bind him hand and foot and throw him out into the outer darkness where there is weeping and gnashing of teeth.' For many are called, but few are chosen."

Then the Pharisees met together to try to think of some way to trap Jesus into saying something for which they could arrest him. They sent secret agents pretending to be honest men to talk with him and try to trap him into saying something he could be arrested for. "Teacher," these spies said, "we know you always tell the truth and don't budge an inch in the face of what others think, but teach the ways of God. Now tell us —is it right to pay taxes to the Roman government or not?"

He saw through their trickery and said, "You hypocrites! Who are you trying to fool with your trick questions? Here, show me a coin." And they handed him a penny. "Whose portrait is this on it? And whose name?"

They replied, "Caesar's—the Roman emperor's."

He said, "Then give the emperor all that is his—and give to God all that is his!" Marveling at his answer, they were silent, and they went away.

That same day, Sadducees, who say there is no resurrection after death, came to him and asked, "Teacher, Moses gave us a law that when a man dies without children, the man's brother should marry his widow and have children in his brother's name. Well, there were seven brothers and the oldest married and died, and left no children. So the second brother married the widow, but soon he died too, and left no children. Then the next brother married her, and died without children, and so on until all were dead, and still there were no children; and last of all, the woman died too. What we want to know is this: In the resurrection, whose wife will she be, for she had been the wife of each of them?"

Jesus replied, "Your trouble is that you don't know the Scriptures, and don't know the power of God. Marriage is for people here on earth, but when those who are counted worthy of being raised from the dead get to heaven, they do not marry. They are like angels, and are sons of God, for they are raised up in new life from the dead.

"But as to your real question—whether or not there is a resurrection—why, even the writings of Moses himself prove this. For when he describes how God appeared to him in the burning bush, he speaks of God as 'the God of Abraham, the

God of Isaac, and the God of Jacob.' God was telling Moses that these men, though dead for hundreds of years, were still very much alive, for he would not have said, 'I *am* the God of those who don't exist! You have made a serious error. God is not the God of the dead, but of the *living*. From God's point of view, all men are living."

Matthew 22: 1–32; Mark 12: 13–27; Luke 20: 20–38.

The Widow's Mite

The Pharisees heard that Jesus had routed the Sadducees with his reply, and one of them, a lawyer, realized that Jesus had answered well. He asked, "Of all the commandments, which is the most important?"

Jesus replied, "The one that says, 'Hear, O Israel! The Lord our God is the one and only God. And you must love him with all your heart and soul and mind and strength.' The second most important is similar: 'Love your neighbor as much as you love yourself.' All the other commandments and all the demands of the prophets stem from these two laws and are fulfilled if you obey them. Keep only these and you will find that you are obeying all the others. No other commandments are greater than these."

The teacher of religion replied, "Sir, you have spoken a true word in saying that there is only one God and no other. And I know it is far more important to love him with all my heart and understanding and strength, and to love others as myself, than to offer all kinds of sacrifices on the altar of the Temple."

Realizing this man's understanding, Jesus said to him, "You are not far from the Kingdom of God."

Then, surrounded by the Pharisees, he asked them a question: "What about the Messiah? Whose son is he?"

"The son of David," they replied.

"Then why does David, speaking under the inspiration of the Holy Spirit, call him 'Lord'?" Jesus asked, "For David said, 'God said to my Lord, Sit at my right hand until I put your enemies beneath your feet.' Since David called him 'Lord,' how can he be merely his son?" They had no answer. And after that no one dared ask him any more questions. (This sort of reasoning delighted the crowd and they listened to him with great interest.)

As Jesus was teaching in the Temple, he asked, "Why do your religious teachers claim that the Messiah must be a descendant of King David? For David himself said in the book of Psalms —and the Holy Spirit was speaking through him when he said it—'God said to my Lord, sit at my right hand until I make your enemies your footstool.' Since David called him his Lord, how can he be his *son?*"

Then, with the crowds listening, he turned to his disciples and said, "Beware of these experts in religion, for they love to parade in dignified robes and to be bowed to by the people as they walk along the street. And how they love the seats of honor in the synagogues and at religious festivals! But even while they are praying long prayers with great outward piety, they are planning schemes to cheat widows out of their property. Therefore God's heaviest sentence awaits these men."

Then he went over to the collection boxes in the Temple and sat and watched as the crowds dropped in their money. Some who were rich put in large amounts. Then a poor widow came and dropped in two pennies. He called his disciples to him and remarked, "Really, this poor widow has given more than all the rest of them combined. For they have given a little of what they didn't need, but she, poor as she is has given everything she has."

Matthew 22: 34–46; Mark 12: 28–44; Luke 20: 41–47; 21: 1–4.

The Greatest Is He Who Serves

To the crowds and to his disciples, Jesus said, "You would think these Jewish leaders and these Pharisees were Moses, the way they keep making up so many laws! And of course you should obey their every whim! It may be all right to do what they say, but above anything else, *don't follow their example.* For they don't do what they tell you to do. They load you with impossible demands that they themselves don't even try to keep.

The Greatest Is He Who Serves

"Everything they do is done for show. They act holy by wearing on their arms little prayer boxes with Scripture verses inside, and by lengthening the memorial fringes of their robes. And how they love to sit at the head table at banquets, and in the reserved pews in the synagogue! How they enjoy the deference paid them on the streets, and to be called 'Rabbi' and 'Master'! Don't ever let anyone call you that. For only God is your Rabbi and all of you are on the same level, as brothers.

"And don't address anyone here on earth as 'Father,' for only God in heaven should be addressed like that. And don't be called 'Master,' for only one is your master, even the Messiah.

"The more lowly your service to others, the greater you are. To be the greatest, be a servant. But those who think themselves great shall be disappointed and humbled; and those who humble themselves shall be exalted.

"Woe to you, Pharisees, and you other religious leaders. Hypocrites! For you won't let others enter the Kingdom of Heaven, and won't go in yourselves. "Yes, woe upon you, Pharisees, and you other religious leaders—hypocrites! For you tithe down to the last mint leaf in your garden, but ignore the important things—justice and mercy and faith. Yes, you should tithe, but you shouldn't leave the more important things undone. Blind guides! You strain out a gnat and swallow a camel.

"Woe to you, Pharisees, and you religious leaders—hypocrites! You are so careful to polish the outside of the cup, but the inside is foul with extortion and greed. Blind Pharisees! First cleanse the inside of the cup, and then the whole cup will be clean.

"Woe to you, Pharisees, and you religious leaders! You are like beautiful mausoleums—full of dead men's bones, and of foulness and corruption. You try to look like saintly men, but underneath those pious robes of yours are hearts besmirched with every sort of hypocrisy and sin.

"Yes, woe to you, Pharisees, and you religious leaders—hypocrites! For you build monuments to the prophets killed by your fathers and lay flowers on the graves of the godly men

131

they destroyed, and say, 'We certainly would never have acted as our fathers did.'

"In saying that, you are accusing yourselves of being the sons of wicked men. And you are following in their steps, filling up the full measure of their evil. Snakes! Sons of vipers! How shall you escape the judgment of hell?

"I will send you prophets, and wise men, and inspired writers, and you will kill some by crucifixion, and rip open the backs of others with whips in your synagogues, and hound them from city to city, so that you will become guilty of all the blood of murdered godly men from righteous Abel to Zechariah (son of Barachiah), slain by you in the Temple between the altar and the sanctuary. Yes, all the accumulated judgment of the centuries shall break upon the heads of this very generation.

"O Jerusalem, Jerusalem, the city that kills the prophets, and stones all those God sends to her! How often I have wanted to gather your children together as a hen gathers her chicks beneath her wings, but you wouldn't let me.

"And now your house is left to you, desolate. For I tell you this, you will never see me again until you are ready to welcome the one sent to you from God."

Matthew 23: 1–39.

Some Greeks who had come to attend the Passover paid a visit to Philip, and said, "Sir, we want to meet Jesus."

Philip and Andrew went together to ask Jesus. Jesus replied that the time had come for him to return to his glory in heaven, and that "I must fall and die like a kernel of wheat that falls into the furrows of the earth. Unless I die I will be alone—a single seed. But my death will produce many new wheat kernels—a plentiful harvest of new lives. If you love your life down here —you will lose it. If you despise your life down here—you will exchange it for eternal glory.

"If these Greeks want to be my disciples, tell them to come and follow me, for my servants must be where I am. And if they follow me, the Father will honor them.

Walk in the Light

"Now my soul is deeply troubled. Shall I pray, 'Father, save me from what lies ahead'? But that is the very reason why I came!

"Father, bring glory and honor to your name."

Then a voice spoke from heaven saying, "I have already done this, and I will do it again."

When the crowd heard the voice, some of them thought it was thunder, while others declared an angel had spoken. Jesus told them, "The voice was for your benefit, not mine. The time of judgment for the world has come—and the time when Satan, the prince of this world, shall be cast out. And when I am lifted up on the cross, I will draw everyone to me." He said this to indicate how he was going to die.

"Die?" asked the crowd. "We understood that the Messiah would live forever and never die. Why are you saying he will die? What Messiah are you talking about?"

John 12: 20–34; 42–50.

Walk in the Light

Jesus replied, "My light will shine out for you just a little while longer. Walk in it while you can, and go where you want to go before the darkness falls, for then it will be too late for you to find your way. Make use of the Light while there is still time; then you will become light bearers."

Many of the Jewish leaders believed Jesus to be the Messiah but wouldn't admit it to anyone because of their fear that the Pharisees would excommunicate them from the synagogue; for they loved the praise of men more than the praise of God.

Jesus shouted to the crowds, "If you trust me, you are really trusting God. For when you see me, you are seeing the one who sent me. I have come as a Light to shine in this dark world, so that all who put their trust in me will no longer wander in the darkness. If anyone hears me and doesn't obey me, I am not his judge—for I have come to save the world, and not to judge it. But all who reject me and my message will be judged at the Day of Judgment by the truths I have spoken. For these are not my own ideas, but I have told you what the Father said to tell you. And I know his instructions lead to eternal life; so whatever he tells me to say, I say!"

John 12: 35, 36; 42–50.

As Jesus was leaving the Temple grounds, his disciples came along and wanted to take him on a tour of the various Temple buildings. One said, "Teacher, what beautiful buildings these are!" Some talked about the beautiful stonework of the Temple and the memorial decorations on the walls.

Jesus replied, "Yes, look! The time is coming when all these things you are admiring will be knocked down, and not one stone will be left on top of another; all will become one vast heap of rubble."

As Jesus sat on the slopes of the Mount of Olives across the valley from Jerusalem, Peter, James, John, and Andrew got alone with him and asked him, "When? And will there be any warning ahead of time? What events will signal your return, and the end of the world?"

So Jesus launched into an extended reply. "Don't let anyone mislead you," he said, "for many will come declaring themselves to be your Messiah, and will lead many astray saying, 'The time has come.' But don't believe them! Don't let anyone mislead you.

"And when you hear of wars and insurrections beginning, don't panic. This does not signal my return; these must come, but the end is not yet. The nations and kingdoms of the earth will rise against each other and there will be famines and epidemics, and great earthquakes in many places, and terrifying things happening in the heavens. All this will be only the beginning of the horrors to come.

"But when these things begin to happen, watch out! For you will be in great danger. Before all this occurs, there will be a time of special persecution, and you will be dragged before the courts, and you will be tortured. You will be beaten in the synagogues, and accused before governors and kings of being my followers. This is your opportunity to tell them the Good News. As a result, the Messiah will be widely known and honored. Then you will be killed and hated all over the world because you are mine."

Matthew 24: 1–9; Mark 13: 1–9; Luke 21: 5–13.

The Gospel for All Nations

"The Good News must first be made known in every nation. But when you are arrested and stand trial, don't worry about what to say in your defense. Just say what God tells you to. Then you will not be speaking, but the Holy Spirit will. Therefore, don't be concerned about how to answer the charges against you, for I will give you the right words and such logic that none of your opponents will be able to reply!

"And many of you shall fall back into sin and betray and hate each other. Even those closest to you—your parents, brothers, relatives, and friends will betray you. Brothers will betray each other to death, fathers will betray their own children, and children will betray their parents to be killed. And everyone will hate you because you are mine. But not a hair of your head will perish! For if you stand firm, you will win your souls.

"And many false prophets will appear and lead many astray. Sin will be rampant everywhere and will cool the love of many. But those enduring to the end shall be saved. And the Good News about the Kingdom will be preached throughout the whole world, so that all nations will hear it, and then, finally, the end will come. So, when you see the horrible thing (told about by Daniel the prophet) standing in a holy place (Note to the reader: You know what is meant!), when you see Jerusalem surrounded by armies, then you will know that the time of its destruction has arrived.

"Then let the people of Judea flee to the hills. Let those in Jerusalem try to escape, and those outside the city must not attempt to return. If you are on your rooftop porch, don't even go back into the house. If you are out in the fields, don't even return for your money or clothes. For those will be days of

135

God's judgment, and the words of the ancient Scriptures written by the prophets will be abundantly fulfilled.

"Woe to expectant mothers in those days, and those with tiny babies. For there will be great distress upon this nation and wrath upon this people. And pray that your flight will not be in winter, or on the Sabbath.* For those will be days of such horror as have never been since the beginning of God's creation, nor will ever be again. And unless the Lord shortens that time of calamity, not a soul in all the earth will survive. But for the sake of his chosen ones he will limit those days. They will be brutally killed by enemy weapons, or sent away as exiles and captives to all the nations of the world; and Jerusalem shall be conquered and trampled down by the Gentiles until the period of Gentile triumph ends in God's good time.

"And then if anyone tells you, 'This is the Messiah,' or, 'That one is,' don't pay any attention, don't believe it. For false Christs shall arise, and false prophets, and will do wonderful miracles, so that if it were possible, even God's chosen ones would be deceived. Take care! I have warned you! So if someone tells you the Messiah has returned and is out in the desert, don't bother to go and look. Or, that he is hiding at a certain place, don't believe it! For as the lightning flashes across the sky from east to west, so shall my coming be, when I, the Messiah, return. And wherever the carcass is, there the vultures will gather.

"Immediately after the tribulation ends there will be strange events in the skies—warnings, evil omens and portents in the sun, moon and stars. The sun will be darkened, and the moon will not give light, and the stars will seem to fall from the heavens, and the powers overshadowing the earth will be convulsed. And down here on earth the nations will be in turmoil, perplexed by the roaring seas and strange tides. The courage of

*The city gates were closed on the Sabbath.

many people will falter because of the fearful fate they see coming upon the earth, for the stability of the very heavens will be broken up."

Mark 13: 10–24; Luke 21: 14–26; Matthew 24: 10–29.

He Will Come with Power

"And then at last the signal of my coming will appear in the heavens and there will be deep mourning all around the earth. And the nations of the world will see me arrive in the clouds of heaven, with power and great glory. And I shall send forth my angels with the sound of a mighty trumpet blast, and they shall gather my chosen ones from the farthest ends of the earth and heaven. So when all these things begin to happen, stand straight and look up! For your salvation is near."

Matthew 24:30, 31; Luke 21: 28.

"Now learn a lesson from the fig tree. Notice the fig tree, or any other tree. When its buds become tender and its leaves begin to sprout, you know without being told that summer is near. In the same way, when you see the events taking place that I've described you can be just as sure that the Kingdom of God is near, even at the doors. I solemnly declare to you that when these things happen, the end of this age has come. Heaven and earth shall pass away, yet my words remain forever.

"However, no one, not even the angels in heaven, nor I myself, knows the day or hour when these things will happen; only the Father knows. And since you don't know when it will happen, stay alert. Be on the watch for my return.

"The world will be at ease—banquets and parties and weddings—just as it was in Noah's time before the sudden coming of the flood; people wouldn't believe what was going to happen until the flood actually arrived and took them all away. So shall my coming be. Two men will be working together in the fields, and one will be taken, the other left. Two women will be going about their household tasks; one will be taken, the other left.

So be prepared, for you don't know what day your Lord is coming.

"My coming can be compared with that of a man who went on a trip to another country. He laid out his employees' work for them to do while he was gone, and told the gatekeeper to watch for his return. Keep a sharp lookout! For you do not know when I will come, at evening, at midnight, early dawn or late daybreak. Don't let me find you sleeping. *Watch for my return!* This is my message to you and to everyone else. Just as a man can prevent trouble from thieves by keeping watch for them, so you can avoid trouble by always being ready for my unannounced return. *Watch for my return!* This is my message to you and to everyone else.

"Are you a wise and faithful servant of the Lord? Have I given you the task of managing my household, to feed my children day by day? Blessings on you if I return and find you faithfully doing your work. I will put such faithful ones in charge of everything I own! But if you are evil and say to yourself, 'My Lord won't be coming for a while,' and begin oppressing your fellow servants, partying and getting drunk, your Lord will arrive unannounced and unexpected, and severely whip you and send you off to the judgment of the hypocrites; there will be weeping and gnashing of teeth.

"The Kingdom of Heaven can be illustrated by the story of ten bridesmaids who took their lamps and went to meet the bridegroom. But only five of them were wise enough to fill their lamps with oil, while the other five were foolish and forgot. So, when the bridegroom was delayed, they lay down to rest until midnight, when they were roused by the shout, 'The bridegroom is coming! Come out and welcome him!' All the girls jumped up and trimmed their lamps. Then the five who hadn't any oil begged the others to share with them, for their lamps were going out. But the others replied, 'We haven't enough. Go instead to the shops and buy some for yourselves.' But while they were gone, the bridegroom came, and those who were ready went in with him to the marriage feast, and the door was locked.

"Later, when the other five returned, they stood outside, calling, 'Sir, open the door for us!' But he called back, 'Go away! It is too late!' So stay awake and be prepared for you do not know the date or moment of my return."

Matthew 24: 32–51; 25: 1–13; Mark 13: 28–37; Luke 21: 29–36.

The Story of the Talents

"Again, the Kingdom of Heaven can be illustrated by the story of a man going into another country, who called together his servants and loaned them money to invest for him while he was gone. He gave $5,000 to one, $2,000 to another, and $1,000 to the last—dividing it in proportion to their abilities—and then left on his trip. The man who received the $5,000 began immediately to buy and sell with it and soon earned another $5,000. The man with $2,000 went right to work, too, and earned another $2,000. But the man who received the $1,000 dug a hole in the ground and hid the money for safe-keeping.

"After a long time their master returned from his trip and called them to him to account for his money. The man to whom he had entrusted the $5,000 brought him $10,000. His master praised him for good work. 'You have been faithful in handling this small amount,' he told him, 'so now I will give you many more responsibilities. Begin the joyous tasks I have assigned to you.' Next came the man who had received the $2,000, with the report, 'Sir, you gave me $2,000 to use, and I have doubled it.' 'Good work,' his master said. 'You are a good and faithful servant. You have been faithful over this small amount, so now I will give you much more.'

"Then the man with the $1,000 came and said, 'Sir, I knew you were a hard man, and I was afraid you would rob me of what I earned, so I hid your money in the earth and here it is!' But his master replied, 'Wicked man! Lazy slave! Since you knew I would demand your profit, you should at least have put my money into the bank so I could have some interest. Take the money from this man and give it to the man with the $10,000. For the man who uses well what he is given shall be given more, and he shall have abundance. But from the man who is unfaithful, even what little responsibility he has shall be taken from him. And throw the useless servant out into outer darkness: there shall be weeping and gnashing of teeth.'

"But when I, the Messiah, shall come in my glory, and all the angels with me, then I shall sit upon my throne of glory. And all the nations shall be gathered before me. And I will separate the people as a shepherd separates the sheep from the goats, and place the sheep at my right hand, and the goats at my left."

Matthew 25: 14–33.

I Was Hungry

"Then I, the King, shall say to those at my right, 'Come, blessed of my Father, into the Kingdom prepared for you from the founding of the world. For I was hungry and you fed me; I was thirsty and you gave me water; I was a stranger and you invited me into your homes; naked and you clothed me; sick and in prison, and you visited me.' Then these righteous ones will reply, 'Sir, when did we ever see you hungry and feed you? Or thirsty and give you anything to drink? Or a stranger, and help you? Or naked, and clothe you? When did we ever see you sick or in prison, and visit you?' And I, the King, will tell them, 'When you did it to these my brothers you were doing it to me!'

"Then I will turn to those on my left and say, 'Away with you, you cursed ones, into the eternal fire prepared for the devil and his demons. For I was hungry and you wouldn't feed me; thirsty, and you wouldn't give me anything to drink; a stranger, and you refused me hospitality; naked, and you wouldn't clothe me; sick, and in prison, and you didn't visit me.' Then they will reply, 'Lord, when did we ever see you hungry or thirsty or a stranger or naked or sick or in prison, and not help you?' And

I Was Hungry

I will answer, 'When you refused to help the least of these my brothers, you were refusing help to me.' And they shall go away into eternal punishment; but the righteous into everlasting life."

Matthew 14: 34–46.

12 Tribulation

"This Woman's Deed Will Be Remembered"

Six days before the Passover ceremonies began, Jesus arrived in Bethany where Lazarus was—the man he had brought back to life. A banquet was prepared in Jesus' honor, in the home of Simon the leper. Martha served, and Lazarus sat at the table with him.

Mary came in with a beautiful flask of expensive perfume made from essence of nard, broke the seal and poured it over his head while he was eating, and anointed Jesus' feet and wiped them with her hair. Some disciples were indignant. "What a waste of good money," they said. Judas Iscariot, the one who would betray him—said, "That perfume was worth a fortune. It should have been sold and the money given to the poor."

Jesus knew what they were thinking and said, "Let her alone; why berate her. She did it in preparation for my burial. You always have the poor among you, and they badly need your help, and you can aid them whenever you want to, but you won't always have me. She has done a good thing to me. She has done what she could. She has poured this perfume on me and has anointed my body ahead of time for burial. Why are you criticizing her? And I tell you this in solemn truth, that wherever the Good News is preached throughout the world, this woman's deed will be remembered and praised."

When the ordinary people of Jerusalem heard of his arrival, they flocked to see him and also to see Lazarus—the man who had come back to life again. Then the chief priests decided to kill Lazarus too, for it was because of him that many of the

Jewish leaders had deserted and believed in Jesus as their Messiah.

John 12: 1–11; Matthew 26: 6–12; Mark 14: 3–9.

The Last Supper

And now the Passover celebration was drawing near—the Jewish festival when only bread made without yeast was used. Every day Jesus went to the Temple to teach, and the crowds began gathering early in the morning to hear him. And each evening he returned to spend the night on the Mount of Olives.

Two days before the feast the chief priests and other Jewish officials were meeting at the residence of Caiaphas the High Priest, to discuss ways of capturing Jesus quietly. "But not during the Passover celebration," they agreed, "for there would be a riot."

Then Judas Iscariot, one of the twelve apostles, went to the chief priests, and asked, "How much will you pay me to get Jesus into your hands?" They were, of course, delighted and promised Judas thirty silver coins. Judas began to look for an opportunity for them to arrest Jesus quietly when the crowds weren't around.

Jesus knew on the evening of Passover Day that it would be his last night on earth before returning to his Father. He told his disciples, "As you know, the Passover celebration begins in two days, and I shall be betrayed and crucified."

Now the day of the Passover celebration arrived, when the Passover lamb was killed and eaten with the unleavened bread. Jesus sent Peter and John ahead to find a place to prepare their Passover meal.

"Where do you want us to go?" they asked.

And he replied, "As soon as you enter Jerusalem, you will see a man walking along carrying a pitcher of water. Follow him into the house he enters. At the house he enters, tell the man in charge, 'Our Master says, my time has come, and I will eat the Passover meal with my disciples at your house. Show us the guest room where he can eat the Passover meal with his disciples.' He will take you upstairs to a large room all ready for us.

143

Go ahead and prepare the meal there." They went and found everything just as Jesus had said, and prepared the Passover supper.

In the evening Jesus arrived with the other disciples, and at the proper time all sat down together at the table; and he said, "I have looked forward to this hour with deep longing, anxious to eat this Passover meal with you before my suffering begins. For I tell you now that I won't eat it again until what it represents has occurred in the Kingdom of God."

Then he took a glass of wine, and when he had given thanks for it, he said, "Take this and share it among yourselves. For I will not drink wine again until the Kingdom of God has come."

He got up from the supper table, took off his robe, wrapped a towel around his loins, poured water into a basin, and began to wash the disciples' feet and to wipe them with the towel. Simon Peter said, "Master, you shouldn't be washing our feet like this!"

Jesus replied, "You don't understand now why I am doing it; some day you will."

"No," Peter protested, "you shall never wash my feet!"

"But if I don't, you can't be my partner," Jesus replied.

Simon Peter exclaimed, "Then wash my hands and head as well—not just my feet!"

Jesus replied, "One who has bathed all over needs only to have his feet washed to be entirely clean. Now you are clean —but that isn't true of everyone here." For Jesus knew who would betray him. That is what he meant when he said, "Not all of you are clean."

After washing their feet he put on his robe again and sat down and asked, "Do you understand what I was doing? You call me 'Master' and 'Lord,' and you do well to say it, for it is true. And since I, the Lord and Teacher, have washed your feet, you ought to wash each other's feet. I have given you an example to follow: do as I have done to you. How true it is that a servant is not greater than his master. Nor is the messenger more important than the one who sends him. You know these things—now do them! That is the path of blessing."

Luke 21: 37–38; 22: 1–18; Matthew 26: 1–5; 14–18; Mark 14: 14, 17; John 13: 2–17.

The Bread and the Wine

On the night when Judas betrayed him, the Lord Jesus took bread, and when he had given thanks and blessed it, he broke it and gave it to his disciples and said, "Take, eat. This is my body, which is given for you. Do this to remember me."

As they were sitting around the table eating, Jesus said, "I solemnly declare that one of you will betray me. Here at this table, sitting among us as a friend, is the man who will betray me. I must die. It is part of God's plan. But, oh, the horror awaiting that man who betrays me. I am not saying these things to all of you; I know so well each one of you I chose. The Scripture declares, 'One who eats supper with me will betray me.' I tell you this now so that when it happens, you will believe on me. Truly, anyone welcoming my messenger is welcoming me. And to welcome me is to welcome the Father who sent me."

Now Jesus was in great anguish of spirit and exclaimed, "Yes, it is true, one of you who is here eating with me will betray me."

The disciples looked at each other, wondering whom he could mean. Sorrow chilled their hearts, and each one asked, one by one, "Am I the one?"

He replied, "It is one of you twelve, the one I served first. I must die, as the prophets declared long ago; but, oh, the misery ahead for the man by whom I am betrayed. Oh, that he had never been born!"

Since I* was sitting next to Jesus at the table, being his closest friend, Simon Peter motioned to me to ask him who it was who would do this terrible deed. So I turned and asked him, "Lord, who is it?"

He told me, "It is the one I honor by giving the bread dipped

---

*Literally, "There was one at the table." All commentators believe him to be John, the writer of this book.

145

in the sauce." And when he had dipped it, he gave it to Judas, son of Simon Iscariot. Jesus told him, "Hurry—do it now."

Judas asked, "Rabbi, am I the one?"

Jesus told him, "Yes." Judas left at once, going out into the night.

As soon as Judas left, Jesus said, "My time has come; the glory of God will soon surround me—and God shall receive great praise because of all that happens to me. And God shall give me his own glory, and this so very soon. Dear, dear children, how brief are these moments before I must go away and leave you! Then, though you search for me, you cannot come to me—just as I told the Jewish leaders.

"I am giving a new commandment to you—love each other just as much as I love you. Your strong love for each other will prove to the world that you are my disciples."

Simon Peter said, "Master, where are you going?"

Jesus replied, "You can't go with me now; but you will follow me later."

Paul: I Corinthians 11: 23, 24; Matthew 26: 22–25; Mark 14: 18–21; Luke 22: 21, 22; John 13: 18–36.

Peter Vows Loyalty to Death

"But why can't I come now?" he asked, "for I am ready to die for you."

Jesus answered, "Die for me? No—three times before the cock crows tomorrow morning, you will deny that you even know me!"

The disciples began to argue among themselves as to who would have the highest rank in the coming Kingdom. Jesus told them, "In this world the kings and great men order their slaves around, and the slaves have no choice but to like it! But among you, the one who serves you best will be your leader. Out in the world the master sits at the table and is served by his servants. But not here! For I am your servant. Nevertheless, because you have stood true to me in these terrible days, and

Peter Vows Loyalty to Death

because my Father has granted me a Kingdom, I, here and now, grant you the right to eat and drink at my table in that Kingdom; and you will sit on thrones judging the twelve tribes of Israel.

"Simon, Simon, Satan has asked to have you, to sift you like wheat, but I have pleaded in prayer for you that your faith should not completely fail. So when you have repented and turned to me again, strengthen and build up the faith of your brothers."

Simon said, "Lord, I am ready to go to jail with you, and even to die with you."

But Jesus said, "Peter, let me tell you something. Between now and tomorrow morning when the rooster crows, you will deny me three times, declaring that you don't even know me."

Then Jesus asked them, "When I sent you out to preach the Good News and you were without money, duffle bag, or extra clothing, how did you get along?"

"Fine," they replied.

"But now," he said, "take a duffle bag if you have one, and your money. And if you don't have a sword, better sell your clothes and buy one! For the time has come for this prophecy about me to come true: 'He will be condemned as a criminal!' Yes, everything written about me by the prophets will come true."

"Master," they replied, "we have two swords among us."

"Enough!" he said.

After supper, in the same way, Jesus took the cup, gave thanks to God for it and gave it to them, saying, "Each one drink from it." And they all drank from it. And he said to them, "This cup is the new agreement between God and you that has been established and set in motion by my blood to save you, and to purchase back your souls, for this is my blood, sealing the New Covenant. It is poured out to forgive the sins of multitudes. Do this in remembrance of me whenever you drink it. Mark my words—I will not drink this wine again until the day

I drink it new with you in the Kingdom of God, my Father's
Kingdom."

*I Corinthians 11: 25; John 13: 37–38; Luke 22: 20, 23–38; Mark 14: 23, 24;
Matthew 26: 27–29.*

The Many Mansions

"Let not your heart be troubled. You are trusting God, now
trust in me. There are many homes up there where my Father
lives, and I am going to prepare them for your coming. When
everything is ready, than I will come and get you, so that you
can always be with me where I am. If this weren't so, I would
tell you plainly. And you know where I am going and how to
get there."

John 14: 1–4.

Peace He Leaves for Us

Thomas said, "We haven't any idea where you are going, so
how can we know the way?"

Jesus told him, "I am the Way—yes, and the Truth and the
Life. No one can get to the Father except by means of me. If you
had known who I am, then you would have known who my
Father is. From now on you know him—and have seen him!"

Philip said, "Sir, show us the Father and we will be satisfied."

Jesus replied, "Don't you even yet know who I am, Philip,
even after all this time I have been with you? Anyone who has
seen me has seen the Father! So why are you asking to see him?
Don't you believe that I am in the Father and the Father is in
me? The words I say are not my own but are from my Father
who lives in me. And he does his work through me. Just believe
it—that I am in the Father and the Father is in me. Or else
believe it because of the mighty miracles you have seen me do.

"In solemn truth I tell you, anyone believing in me shall do
the same miracles I have done, and even greater ones, because
I am going to be with the Father. You can ask him for *anything,*
using my name, and I will do it, for this will bring praise to the
Father because of what I, the Son, will do for you. Yes, ask
anything, using my name, and I will do it!

Peace He Leaves for Us

"If you love me, obey me; and I will ask the Father and he will give you another Comforter, and he will never leave you. He is the Holy Spirit, the Spirit who leads into all truth. The world at large cannot receive him, for it isn't looking for him and doesn't recognize him. But you do, for he lives with you now and some day shall be in you. No, I will not abandon you or leave you as orphans in the storm—I will come to you. In just a little while I will be gone from the world, but I will still be present with you. For I will live again—and you will too. When I come back to life again, you will know that I am in my Father, and you in me, and I in you. The one who obeys me is the one who loves me; and because he loves me, my Father will love him; and I will too, and I will reveal myself to him."

Judas (not Judas Iscariot, but his other disciple with that name) said to him, "Sir, why are you going to reveal yourself only to us disciples and not to the world at large?"

Jesus replied, "Because I will only reveal myself to those who love me and obey me. The Father will love them too, and we will come to them and live with them. Anyone who doesn't obey me doesn't love me. And remember, I am not making up this answer to your question! It is the answer given by the Father who sent me. I am telling you these things now while I am still with you. But when the Father sends the Comforter instead of me—and by the Comforter I mean the Holy Spirit— he will teach you much, as well as remind you of everything I myself have told you.

"I am leaving you with a gift—peace of mind and heart! And the peace I give isn't fragile like the peace the world gives. So don't be troubled or afraid. Remember what I told you—I am going away, but I will come back to you again. If you really love me, you will be very happy for me, for now I can go to the Father, who is greater than I am. I have told you these things before they happen so that when they do, you will believe in me.

"I don't have much more time to talk to you, for the evil prince of this world approaches. He has no power over me, but

I will freely do what the Father requires of me so that the world will know that I love the Father."

John 14: 5–31.

The True Vine

"I am the true Vine, and my Father is the Gardener. He lops off every branch that doesn't produce. And he prunes those branches that bear fruit for even larger crops. He has already tended you by pruning you back for greater strength and usefulness by means of the commands I gave you. Take care to live in me, and let me live in you. For a branch can't produce fruit when severed from the vine. Nor can you be fruitful apart from me.

"Yes, I am the Vine; you are the branches. Whoever lives in me, and I in him shall produce a large crop of fruit. For apart from me you can't do a thing. If anyone separates from me, he is thrown away like a useless branch, withers, and is gathered into a pile with all the others and burned. But if you stay in me and obey my commands, you may ask any request you like, and it will be granted! My true disciples produce bountiful harvests. This brings great glory to my Father.

"I have loved you even as the Father has loved me. Live within my love. When you obey me you are living in my love, just as I obey my Father and live in his love. I have told you this so that you will be filled with my joy. Yes, your cup of joy will overflow! I demand that you love each other as much as I love you."

John 15: 1–12.

Greater Love Hath No Man

"And here is how to measure it—the greatest love is shown when a person lays down his life for his friends; and you are my friends if you obey me. I no longer call you slaves, for a master doesn't confide in his slaves; now you are my friends, proved by the fact that I have told you everything the Father told me.

"You didn't choose me! I chose you! I appointed you to go

and produce lovely fruit always, so that no matter what you ask for from the Father, using my name, he will give it to you. I demand that you love each other, for you get enough hate from the world! But then, it hated me before it hated you. The world would love you if you belonged to it; but you don't—for I chose you to come out of the world, and so it hates you. Do you remember what I told you? 'A slave isn't greater than his master!' So since they persecuted me, naturally they will persecute you. And if they had listened to me, they would listen to you! The people of the world will persecute you because you belong to me, for they don't know God who sent me.

"They would not be guilty if I had not come and spoken to them. But now they have no excuse for their sin. Anyone hating me is also hating my Father. If I hadn't done such mighty miracles among them they would not be counted guilty. But as it is, they saw these miracles and yet they hated both of us— me and my Father. This has fulfilled what the prophets said concerning the Messiah, 'They hated me without reason.'

"But I will send you the Comforter—the Holy Spirit, the source of all truth. He will come to you from the Father and will tell you all about me. And you also must tell everyone about me, because you have been with me from the beginning.

"I have told you these things so that you won't be staggered by all that lies ahead."

John 15: 13–27; 16: 1.

"For you will be excommunicated from the synagogues, and indeed the time is coming when those who kill you will think they are doing God a service. This is because they have never known the Father or me. Yes, I'm telling you these things now so that when they happen you will remember I warned you. I didn't tell you earlier because I was going to be with you for a while longer.

"But now I am going away to the one who sent me; and none of you seems interested in the purpose of my going; none wonders why. Instead you are only filled with sorrow. But the fact of the matter is that it is best for you that I go away, for if I don't, the Comforter won't come. If I do, he will—for I will send him to you.

"And when he has come he will convince the world of its sin, and of the availability of God's goodness, and of deliverance from judgment. The world's sin is unbelief in me; there is righteousness available because I go to the Father and you shall see me no more; there is deliverance from judgment because the prince of this world has already been judged.

"Oh, there is so much more I want to tell you, but you can't understand it now. When the Holy Spirit, who is truth, comes, he shall guide you into all truth, for he will not be presenting his own ideas, but will be passing on to you what he has heard. He will tell you about the future. He shall praise me and bring me great honor by showing you my glory. All the Father's glory is mine; this is what I mean when I say that he will show you my glory. In just a little while I will be gone, and you will see me no more; but just a little while after that, and you will see me again!"

"Whatever is he saying?" some of his disciples asked. "What is this about 'going to the Father'? We don't know what he means."

Jesus realized they wanted to ask him so he said, "Are you asking yourselves what I mean? The world will greatly rejoice over what is going to happen to me, and you will weep. But your weeping shall suddenly be turned to wonderful joy when you see me again. It will be the same joy as that of a woman in labor when her child is born—her anguish gives place to rapturous joy and the pain is forgotten. You have sorrow now, but I will see you again and then you will rejoice; and no one can rob you of that joy. At that time you won't need to ask me for anything, for you can go directly to the Father and ask him, and he will give you what you ask for because you use my name. You haven't tried this before, but begin now. Ask, using my name, and you will receive, and your cup of joy will overflow.

Trouble!—But It Can Be Overcome

"I have spoken of these matters very guardedly, but the time will come when this will not be necessary and I will tell you plainly all about the Father. Then you will present your petitions over my signature! And I won't need to ask the Father to grant these requests, for the Father himself loves you dearly because you love me and believe that I came from the Father. Yes, I came from the Father into the world and will leave the world and return to the Father."

"At last you are speaking plainly," his disciples said, "and not in riddles. Now we understand that you know everything. From this we believe that you came from God."

"Do you finally believe this?" Jesus asked. "But the time is coming—in fact, it is here—when you will be scattered, each one returning to his own home, leaving me alone. Yet I will not be alone, for the Father is with me."

John 16: 2–32.

Trouble!—But It Can Be Overcome

"I have told you all this so that you will have peace of heart and mind. Here on earth you will have many trials and sorrows; but cheer up, for I have overcome the world."

When Jesus had finished saying all these things he looked up to heaven and said, "Father, the time has come. Reveal the glory of your Son so that he can give the glory back to you. For you have given him authority over every man and woman in all the earth. He gives eternal life to each one you have given him. And this is the way to have eternal life—by knowing you, the only true God, and Jesus Christ, the one you sent to earth! I brought glory to you here on earth by doing everything you told me to. And now, Father, reveal my glory as I stand in your presence, the glory we shared before the world began.

"I have told these men all about you. They were in the world, but then you gave them to me. Actually, they were always yours, and you gave them to me; and they have obeyed you. Now they know that everything I have is a gift from you, for

153

I have passed on to them the commands you gave me; and they accepted them and know of a certainty that I came down to earth from you, and they believe you sent me.

"My plea is not for the world but for those you have given me because they belong to you. And all of them, since they are mine, belong to you; and you have given them back to me with everything else of yours, and so *they are my glory!* Now I am leaving the world, and leaving them behind, and coming to you. Holy Father, keep them in your own care—all those you have given me—so that they will be united just as we are, with none missing. During my time here I have kept safe within your family all of these you gave me. I guarded them so that not one perished, except the son of hell, as the Scriptures foretold.

"And now I am coming to you. I have told them many things while I was with them so that they would be filled with my joy. I have given them your commands. And the world hates them because they don't fit in with it, just as I don't. I'm not asking you to take them out of the world, but to keep them safe from Satan's power. They are not part of this world any more than I am. Make them pure and holy through teaching them your words of truth. As you sent me into the world, I am sending them into the world, and I consecrate myself to meet their need for growth in truth and holiness.

"I am not praying for these alone but also for the future believers who will come to me because of the testimony of these. My prayer for all of them is that they will be of one heart and mind, just as you and I are, Father—that just as you are in me and I am in you, so they will be in us, and the world will believe you sent me.

"I have given them the glory you gave me—the glorious unity of being one, as we are—I in them and you in me, all being perfected into one—so that the world will know you sent me and will understand that you love them as much as you love me. Father, I want them with me—these you've given me—so that they can see my glory. You gave me the glory because you loved me before the world began!

Trouble!—But It Can Be Overcome

"O righteous Father, the world doesn't know you, but I do; and these disciples know you sent me. And I have revealed you to them, and will keep on revealing you so that the mighty love you have for me may be in them, and I in them.

"Come, let's be going."

John 16: 33; 17: 1–26; 14: 31.

13 Gethsemane

Before the Cock Crows Twice

When they had sung a hymn, Jesus left the upstairs room and went as usual to the Mount of Olives, accompanied by the disciples. Then Jesus said to them, "Tonight you will all desert me. For it is written in the Scriptures that God will smite the Shepherd and the sheep of the flock will be scattered. But after I have been brought back to life again I will go to Galilee, and meet you there."

Peter declared, "If everyone else deserts you, I won't. I will never desert you no matter what the others do!"

Jesus told him, "The truth is that this very night, before the cock crows a second time tomorrow morning you will deny me three times."

"No!" Peter exploded. "Not even if I have to die with you! I'll *never* deny you!" And all the others vowed the same.

Jesus crossed the Kidron ravine with his disciples and entered a grove of olive trees, called the Garden of Gethsemane, and he instructed his disciples, "Sit here, while I go and pray. Pray God that you will not be overcome by temptation." He walked away, perhaps a stone's throw, taking Peter, James and John with him. He said to them, "My soul is crushed by sorrow to the point of death; stay here and watch with me."

He went on a little further, knelt down and prayed this prayer: "Father, Father, everything is possible for you. Father! If it is possible, if you are willing, please take away this cup of horror from me. But I want your will, not mine."

Before the Cock Crows Twice

He was in such agony of spirit that he broke into a sweat of blood, with great drops falling to the ground.

He returned to the three disciples and found them asleep. "Peter," he called, "couldn't you even stay awake with me one hour? Keep alert and pray. Otherwise temptation will overpower you. For the spirit indeed is willing, but how weak the body is!"

Again he left them and prayed, "My Father! If it is possible, let this cup be taken away from me. If this cup cannot go away until I drink it all, your will be done."

He stood up again and returned to the disciples—only to find them asleep, exhausted from grief. "Asleep!" he said. "Get up! Pray God that you will not fall when you are tempted."

He went back to prayer the third time, saying the same things again. "Father, take away this cup from me. Yet I want your will, not mine." The third time when he returned he again found them sleeping, and said, "Sleep on now and take your rest . . . but no! The time has come! I am betrayed into the hands of evil men! Up! Let's be going! Look! Here comes the man who is betraying me!

Judas knew this place, for Jesus had gone there many times with his disciples. Immediately, while he was still speaking, Judas arrived with a mob, sent out by the chief priests and other Jewish leaders, with blazing torches, lanterns, and equipped with swords and clubs.

Jesus fully realized all that was going to happen to him. Stepping forward to meet them he asked, "Whom are you looking for?"

"Jesus of Nazareth," they replied.

"I am he," Jesus said. They all fell backwards to the ground! Once more he asked them, "Whom are you searching for?"

They replied, "Jesus of Nazareth."

"I told you I am he," Jesus said; "and since I am the one you are after, let these others go." He did this to carry out the prophecy he had just made, "I have not lost a single one of those you gave me . . ."

Matthew 26: 30–46; Mark 14: 29–43; Luke 22: 39–46; John 18: 1–9.

Judas Betrays Him

Judas had told them, "You will know which one to arrest when I go over and greet him." Judas walked up to Jesus. "Master!" he exclaimed, and embraced him with a great show of friendliness.

Jesus said, "My friend, go ahead and do what you have come for. Judas, how can you do this—betray the Messiah with a kiss?" Then the others grabbed him.

The disciples exclaimed, "Master, shall we fight? We brought along the swords!" Simon Peter drew a sword and slashed off the right ear of Malchus, the High Priest's servant.

Jesus said, "Don't resist any more." And he touched the place where the man's ear had been and restored it. "Put away your sword," Jesus told him. "Those using swords will get killed. Shall I not drink from the cup the Father has given me? Don't you realize that I could ask my Father for thousands of angels to protect us, and he would send them instantly? But if I did, how would the Scriptures be fulfilled that describe what is happening now?"

Then Jesus spoke to the crowd. "Am I some dangerous criminal," he asked, "that you had to arm yourselves with swords and clubs before you could arrest me? I was with you teaching daily in the Temple and you didn't stop me then. Why didn't you arrest me in the Temple? But this is your moment—the time when Satan's power reigns supreme. This is all happening to fulfill the words of the prophets as recorded in the Scriptures, to fulfill the prophecies about me."

At that point, all the disciples deserted him and fled. The Jewish police tied Jesus and led him to the High Priest's residence (Caiaphas, that year). Simon Peter followed to see what was going to be done to Jesus, and so did another of the disciples who was acquainted with the High Priest. That other disciple was permitted into the courtyard along with Jesus, while

The Prejudged Trial

Peter stood outside the gate. The other disciple spoke to the girl watching at the gate, and she let Peter in.

The soldiers lit a fire in the courtyard. Peter stood there with the household servants warming himself.

The entire Jewish Supreme Court assembled with Caiaphas, the High Priest. The High Priest asked Jesus about his followers and what he had been teaching them. Jesus replied, "What I teach is widely known, for I have preached regularly in the synagogue and Temple; I have been heard by all the Jewish leaders and teach nothing in private that I have not said in public. Why are you asking me this question?"

One of the soldiers standing there struck Jesus with his fist. "Is that the way to answer the High Priest?" he demanded.

"If I lied, prove it," Jesus replied. "Should you hit a man for telling the truth?"

Matthew 26: 50–59; Mark 14: 44–49; 54; Luke 22: 48–55; John 18: 10–23.

The Prejudged Trial

The chief priests and the whole Jewish Supreme Court were trying to find something against Jesus that would be sufficient to condemn him to death. Many false witnesses volunteered, but they contradicted each other. Finally two men were found who declared, "We heard him say, 'I will destroy the Temple of God, made with human hands, and in three days I will build another, made without human hands!'"

The High Priest stood up and said to Jesus, "Well, what about it?" But Jesus remained silent. The High Priest said, "Tell us whether you claim to be the Messiah, the Son of God."

"Yes," Jesus said, "I am. In the future you will see me, the Messiah, sitting at the right hand of God and returning on the clouds of heaven."

Then the High Priest said, "You have heard his blasphemy. What need have we for other witnesses? What is your verdict?" And the vote for the death sentence was unanimous.

They blindfolded Jesus and hit him with their fists and asked, "Who hit you that time, prophet?"

Meanwhile Peter was below in the courtyard. The girl watching at the gate noticed him in the firelight and began staring at him, and then announced, *"You* were with Jesus of Galilee."

Peter denied it. He said, "I don't even know the man. I don't know what you're talking about!" and walked over to the edge of the courtyard. Just then, a rooster crowed.

After a while someone else looked at him and said, "You must be one of them, for you are from Galilee, we can tell by your Galilean accent."

"No sir, I am not!" Peter replied.

About an hour later someone else flatly stated, "I know this fellow is one of Jesus' disciples."

Peter began to swear. "I don't even know this fellow you are talking about," he said. And immediately the rooster crowed the second time. Suddenly Jesus' words flashed through Peter's mind: "Before the cock crows twice, you will deny me three times." And he began to cry.

Early the next morning at daybreak the Jewish Supreme Court assembled, including the chief priests and all the top religious authorities of the nation. Jesus was led before this Council, and instructed to state whether or not he claimed to be the Messiah. He replied, "If I tell you, you won't believe me or let me present my case. But the time is soon coming when I, the Messiah, shall be enthroned beside Almighty God."

They all shouted, "Then you claim you are the Son of God?"

And he replied, "Yes, I am."

They said, "We ourselves have heard him say it."

The chief priests and Jewish leaders met again to discuss how to sentence Jesus to death.

Judas, when he saw that Jesus had been condemned to die, deeply regretted what he had done, and brought back the money to the chief priests. "I have sinned," he declared, "for I have betrayed an innocent man."

"That's your problem," they retorted. Then he threw the money onto the floor of the Temple and went out and hanged himself.

The chief priests picked the money up. "We can't put it in

the collection," they said, "since it's against our laws to accept money paid for murder." They talked it over and finally decided to buy a certain field where the clay was used by potters, and to make it into a cemetery for foreigners who died in Jerusalem.

Matthew 26: 60–73; 27: 1–7; Mark 14: 55–73; Luke 22: 56–71; John 18: 16.

Christ Before Pilate—Behold the Man

The entire Council took Jesus away from the High Priest Caiaphas over to the palace of the Roman Governor, Pontius Pilate. Pilate, the governor, went out to them and said, "Take him away and judge him yourselves by your own laws."

"But we want him crucified," they demanded, "and your approval is required." Then Pilate went back into the palace and called for Jesus to be brought to him.

"Are you the King of the Jews?" he asked him.

" 'King' as *you* use the word or as the *Jews* use it?" Jesus asked.

"Am I a Jew?" Pilate retorted. "Your own people brought you here. Why? What have you done?"

Jesus answered, "I am not an earthly king. If I were, my followers would have fought when I was arrested by the Jewish leaders. But my Kingdom is not of the world."

Pilate replied, "But you are a king then?"

"Yes," Jesus said, "I was born for that purpose. And I came to bring truth to the world. All who love the truth are my followers."

"What is truth?" Pilate exclaimed. Then he went out again to the people and told them, "He is not guilty of any crime. But you have a custom of asking me to release someone from prison each year at Passover. So if you want me to, I'll release the 'King of the Jews.' "

But they screamed back, "No! Not this man, but Barabbas!" Barabbas was a robber.

The chief priests and Jewish officials began yelling, "Crucify! Crucify!"

"You crucify him," Pilate said. "I find him *not guilty.*"

They replied, "By our laws he ought to die because he called himself the Son of God."

When Pilate heard this, he asked him, "Where are you from?" but Jesus gave no answer. "You won't talk to me?" Pilate demanded. "Don't you realize that I have the power to release you or to crucify you?"

Jesus said, "You would have no power at all over me unless it were given to you from above. So those who brought me to you have the greater sin."

Then Pilate tried to release him, but the Jewish leaders told him, "This fellow has been telling our people not to pay their taxes to the Roman government and claiming he is our Messiah—a King. If you release this man, you are no friend of Caesar's. Anyone who declares himself a king is a rebel against Caesar."

Pilate asked him, "Are you their Messiah—their King?"

"Yes," Jesus replied, "it is as you say."

The chief priests accused him of many crimes, and Pilate asked him, "Why don't you say something? What about all these charges against you? Don't you hear what they are saying?" But Jesus said nothing, much to the governor's surprise. Pilate turned to the mob and said, "That isn't a crime!"

Then they became desperate. "But he is causing riots against the government everywhere he goes, all over Judea, from Galilee to Jerusalem!"

"Is he then a Galilean?" Pilate asked. When they told him yes, Pilate said to take him to King Herod, for Galilee was under Herod's jurisdiction; and Herod happened to be in Jerusalem at the time.

Herod was delighted for he had heard a lot about Jesus and had been hoping to see him perform a miracle. He asked Jesus question after question, but there was no reply. Herod sent him back to Pilate.

John 18: 28-40; 19: 6-12; Luke 23: 1-11; Mark 15: 3, 4; Matthew 27: 13, 14.

Pilate Washes His Hands

Pilate called together the chief priests and other Jewish leaders, and announced his verdict: "You brought this man to me, accusing him of leading a revolt against the Roman government. I have examined him thoroughly on this point and find him innocent. Herod came to the same conclusion."

Now the governor's custom was to release one Jewish prisoner each year during the Passover celebration—anyone they wanted. As the crowds gathered before Pilate's house that morning he asked them, "Which shall I release to you—Barabbas, or Jesus your Messiah?"

A mighty roar rose from the crowd, "Release Barabbas to us!"

"Then what shall I do with Jesus?" Pilate asked.

And they shouted, "Crucify him!"

"What? Crucify your king?" Pilate asked.

"We have no king but Caesar," the chief priests shouted back.

When Pilate saw that he wasn't getting anywhere, he sent for a bowl of water and washed his hands before the crowd saying, "I am innocent of the blood of this good man. The responsibility is yours!"

And the mob yelled back, "His blood be on us and on our children!"

Then Pilate, anxious to please the people, sentenced Jesus to die as they demanded. He released Barabbas, the man in prison for insurrection and murder. He ordered Jesus flogged with a leaded whip, and handed him over to be crucified.

Luke 23: 13–25; Matthew 27: 15–17; John 19: 15, 22–25; Mark 15: 15.

"Father, Forgive Them"

The Roman soldiers took Jesus into the armory, the barracks of the palace. They stripped him and dressed him in a purple robe and made a crown from long thorns and put it on his head.

Then Jesus came out wearing the crown of thorns and the

purple robe. They knelt before him in mockery yelling, "Hail, King of the Jews."

After the mockery, they took off the robe and put his own garment on him again, struck him with their fists, and took him out to crucify him.

Great crowds trailed along behind, and many grief-stricken women. But Jesus turned and said to them, "Daughters of Jerusalem, don't weep for me, but for yourselves and for your children. For the days are coming when the women who have no children will be counted fortunate indeed. Mankind will beg the mountains to fall on them and crush them, and the hills to bury them. For if such things as this are done to me, the Living Tree, what will they do to you?"

He was taken out of the city, carrying his cross.

As they were on the way to the execution grounds they came across a man, Simon of Cyrene, who was coming in from the country just then. Simon was pressed into service, forced to follow, carrying Jesus' cross.

Two others, criminals, were led out to be executed with him. They went out to an area known as "The Skull," in Hebrew, "Golgotha," where the soldiers gave him drugged wine to drink; but when he had tasted it, he refused. It was about nine o'clock in the morning.

There all three were crucified—Jesus on the center cross, and the two criminals on either side.

"Father, forgive these people," Jesus said, "for they don't know what they are doing." Pilate posted a sign over him reading, in Hebrew, Latin, and Greek, "Jesus of Nazareth, the King of the Jews."

Matthew 27: 26–34; Mark 15: 16–25; Luke 23: 26–34; John 19: 3–5, 17–20.

When the soldiers had crucified Jesus, they put his garments into four piles, one for each of them, and threw dice for his clothes.

The people jeered at him as they walked by, and wagged their heads in mockery. "Ha! Look at you now!" they yelled at him.

Jesus Remembers Everyone

"Sure, you can destroy the Temple and rebuild it in three days! If you're so wonderful, save yourself."

The soldiers mocked him, too. They called to him, "If you are the King of the Jews, save yourself!"

The chief priests and religious leaders were also standing around joking about Jesus. "He's quite clever at 'saving' others," they said, "but he can't save himself!"

One of the criminals hanging beside him also threw the same in his teeth. But the other criminal protested, "Don't you even fear God? We deserve to die for our evil deeds, but this man hasn't done one thing wrong."

Matthew 27: 39–44; Mark 15: 24, 29–31; Luke 23: 36–41; John 19: 23.

Jesus Remembers Everyone

Then he said, "Jesus, remember me when you come into your Kingdom."

And Jesus replied, "Today you will be with me in Paradise. This is a solemn promise."

Standing near the cross were Jesus' mother, Mary, his aunt, the wife of Cleopas, and Mary Magdalene. When Jesus saw his mother standing there beside a disciple, John, his close friend, he said to her, "He is your son." And to the disciple he said, "She is your mother!" And from then on that disciple took her into his home.

That afternoon, the whole earth was covered with darkness for three hours, from noon until three o'clock. About three o'clock, Jesus called out with a loud voice, "My God, my God, why have you deserted me?"

Jesus knew that everything was now finished, and to fulfill the Scriptures said, "I'm thirsty." One of them ran and filled a sponge with sour wine and put it on a hyssop branch, a stick, and held it up to Jesus' lips. When Jesus had tasted it, he said, "It is finished."

Jesus shouted out again, "Father, I commit my spirit to you," and with those words he bowed his head, dismissed his spirit, and died.

Jesus' friends stood in the distance watching. Some women were there watching also—Mary Magdalene, Mary (the mother of James the Younger and of Joses), Salome, the mother of James and John (the sons of Zebedee), and many other Galilean women who had come with him to Jerusalem.

Matthew 27: 45–56; Mark 15: 34, 40, 41; Luke 23: 42–49; John 19: 25–30.

14 Victory

The Tomb

This all happened the day before the Sabbath. Late that afternoon Joseph from Arimathea, being a secret disciple of Jesus for fear of the Jewish leaders, went to Pilate and asked for Jesus' body. Joseph was a rich man from Arimathea in Judea, an honored member of the Jewish Supreme Court, a godly man who had not agreed with the decision and actions of the other Jewish leaders. He was personally eagerly expecting the arrival of God's Kingdom.

Joseph boldly asked Pilate for permission to take Jesus' body down; and Pilate told him to go ahead. So he came and took it away. Nicodemus, the man who had come to Jesus at night, came too, bringing embalming ointment made from myrrh and aloes. Together they wrapped Jesus' body in a long, clean linen cloth saturated with the spices, as is the Jewish custom of burial. The place of crucifixion was near a grove of trees, where there was a new tomb, never used before. Joseph placed the body in his own new rock-hewn tomb, and rolled a great stone across the entrance as he left.

The women from Galilee saw it carried into the tomb. Both Mary Magdalene and the other Mary, the mother of Joses, were sitting nearby watching. Then they went home and prepared spices and ointments to embalm him; but by the time they were finished it was the Sabbath, so they rested all that day as required by the Jewish law.

The next day—at the close of the first day of the Passover ceremonies—the chief priests and Pharisees went to Pilate, and told him, "Sir, that liar once said, 'After three days I will come back to life again.' So we request an order from you sealing the tomb until the third day, to prevent his disciples from coming and stealing his body and then telling everyone he came back to life! If that happens we'll be worse off than we were at first."

"Use your own Temple police," Pilate told them. "They can guard it safely enough." So they sealed the stone and posted guards to protect it from intrusion.

Mark 15: 42, 43; Luke 23: 52–56; John 19: 38–41; Matthew 27: 57–66.

The First Easter Morning

Early on Sunday morning, as the new day was dawning, Mary Magdalene, the other Mary, and Salome went out to the tomb. They carried embalming spices with them. On the way they were discussing how they could ever roll aside the huge stone from the entrance, but found that the huge stone covering the entrance had been rolled aside. So they went in—but the Lord Jesus' body was gone. They stood there puzzled.

Suddenly two men appeared before them, clothed in shining robes so bright their eyes were dazzled. The men asked, "Why are you looking in a tomb for someone who is alive? He isn't here! He has come back to life again! Don't you remember what he told you back in Galilee—that the Messiah must be betrayed into the power of evil men and be crucified and that he would rise again the third day?"

Then the women remembered, and fled from the tomb, trembling but also filled with joy, and rushed to find the disciples to give them the angels' message.

Suddenly Jesus was there in front of them! "Good morning!" he said. And they worshipped him. Then Jesus said to them, "Don't be frightened! Go tell my brothers to leave at once for Galilee, to meet me there."

Later, Mary Magdalene returned to the tomb and was standing outside, crying. She glanced over her shoulder and saw someone standing behind her. It was Jesus, but she didn't recognize him.

"Why are you crying?" he asked her. "Whom are you look-ing for?"

She thought he was the gardener. "Sir," she said, "if you have taken him away, tell me where you have put him, and I will go and get him."

"Mary!" Jesus said. She turned toward him.

"Master!" she exclaimed.

"Don't touch me," he cautioned, "for I haven't yet ascended to the Father. But go find my brothers and tell them that I ascend to my Father and your Father, my God and your God."

Mary Magdalene found the disciples and told them, "I have seen the Lord! And he is alive!" Then she gave them his mes-sage. But they didn't believe her!

Matthew 28: 1, 8–10; Mark 16: 1–11; Luke 24: 1–9; John 20: 11–18.

He Met Them on the Dusty Road

Later that day he appeared to two of his followers but they didn't recognize him because he had changed his appearance. They were walking to the village of Emmaus, seven miles out of Jerusalem.

As they were talking of Jesus' death, Jesus himself came along and joined them. But they didn't recognize him, for God kept them from it. "You seem to be in a deep discussion about something," he said. "What are you so concerned about?" They stopped short, sadness written across their faces.

One of them, Cleopas replied, "You must be the only person in Jerusalem who hasn't heard about the terrible things that happened there last week."

"What things?" Jesus asked.

"The things that happened to Jesus, the Man from Nazareth," they said. "Our religious leaders crucified him. We had thought he was the glorious Messiah and that he had come to rescue Israel."

Jesus said to them, "You are such foolish, foolish people! You find it so hard to believe all that the prophets wrote in the Scriptures! Wasn't it clearly predicted by the prophets that the Messiah would have to suffer all these things before entering his time of glory?" Then Jesus quoted them passage after passage from the writings of the prophets, beginning with the book of Genesis and going right on through the Scriptures, explaining what the passages meant and what they said about himself.

By this time they were nearing Emmaus and the end of their journey. Jesus would have gone on, but they begged him to stay the night with them, as it was getting late. So he went home with them. As they sat down to eat, he asked God's blessing on the food and then took a small loaf of bread and broke it and was passing it over to them, when suddenly—it was as though their eyes were opened—they recognized him! And at that moment he disappeared!

Within the hour they were on their way back to Jerusalem, where the eleven disciples greeted them with these words, "The Lord has really risen! He appeared to Peter!" Then the two from Emmaus told their story of how Jesus had appeared to them as they were walking along the road and how they had recognized him as he was breaking the bread.

That evening the disciples were meeting behind locked doors, in fear of the Jewish leaders, when suddenly Jesus was standing there among them! He greeted them. But the whole group was terribly frightened, thinking they were seeing a ghost!

"Why are you frightened?" he asked. "Why do you doubt that it is really I? Look at my hands! Look at my feet! You can see that it is I, myself! Touch me and make sure that I am not a ghost! For ghosts don't have bodies, as you see that I do!" Still they stood there, filled with doubt.

He asked, "Do you have anything here to eat?" They gave him a piece of fish, and he ate it as they watched!

He spoke to them again and said, "As the Father has sent me, even so I am sending you." Then he breathed on them and told them, "Receive the Holy Spirit. If you forgive anyone's sins, they are forgiven. If you refuse to forgive them, they are unforgiven."

Mark 16: 12; Luke 24: 13–31; 33–43; John 20: 19–23.

Thomas Feels the Print of the Nails

Thomas was not there at the time. When they kept telling him, "We have seen the Lord," he replied, "I won't believe it unless I see the nail wounds in his hands—and put my fingers into them—and place my hand into his side."

Eight days later the disciples were together again, and this time Thomas was with them. The doors were locked; but suddenly, as before, Jesus was standing among them and greeting them. Then he said to Thomas, "Put your finger into my hands. Put your hand into my side. Don't be faithless any longer. Believe!"

"My Lord and my God!" Thomas said.

Then Jesus told him, "You believe because you have seen me. But blessed are those who haven't seen me and believe anyway."

John 20: 24–29.

John Is Speaking

Jesus appeared again to the disciples beside the Lake of Galilee. This is how it happened:

A group of us were there—Simon Peter, Thomas, "The Twin," Nathanael from Cana in Galilee, my brother James and I and two other disciples. Simon Peter said, "I'm going fishing."

"We'll come too," we all said. We did, but caught nothing all night.

At dawn we saw a man standing on the beach but couldn't see who he was. He called, "Any fish, boys?"

"No," we replied.

Then he said, "Throw out your net on the right-hand side of the boat, and you'll get plenty of them!" So we did.

When we got to land, we saw that a fire was kindled and fish were frying over it, and there was bread. "Bring some of the fish you've just caught," Jesus said. Peter dragged the net ashore. There were 153 large fish; and yet the net hadn't torn.

Then I said to Peter, "It is the Lord."

"Now come and have some breakfast!" Jesus said. Jesus went around serving us the bread and fish.

John 21: 1–14.

Feed My Sheep and Follow Me

After breakfast Jesus said, "Simon, son of John, do you love me more than these others?"

"Yes," Peter replied, "You know I am your friend."

"Then feed my lambs," Jesus told him. Jesus repeated the question: "Simon, son of John do you *really* love me?"

"Yes, Lord," Peter said, "you know I am your friend."

"Then take care of my sheep," Jesus said. Once more he asked him, "Simon, son of John, are you even my friend?"

Peter was grieved at the way Jesus asked the question this third time. "Lord, you know my heart; you know I am," he said.

Jesus said, "Then feed my little sheep. When you were young, you were able to do as you liked and go wherever you wanted to; but when you are old, you will stretch out your hands and others will direct you and take you where you don't want to go." Jesus said this to let him know what kind of death he would die to glorify God. Then Jesus told him, "Follow me."

Peter turned around and saw the disciple Jesus loved. Peter asked Jesus, "What about him, Lord? What sort of death will he die?" Jesus replied, "If I want him to live until I return, what is that to you? *You* follow me."

I am that disciple! I saw these events and have recorded them here. And we all know that my account of these things is accurate. And I suppose that if all the other events in Jesus' life were written, the whole world could hardly contain the books!

John 21: 15–25.

The eleven disciples left for Galilee, going to the mountain where Jesus had said they would find him. There they met him, and he told them, "You are to go into all the world and preach the Good News to everyone, everywhere. Those who believe and are baptized will be saved. But those who refuse to believe will be condemned.

"And those who believe shall use my authority to cast out demons, and they shall speak new languages. They will be able even to handle snakes with safety, and if they drink anything poisonous, it won't hurt them; and they will be able to place their hands on the sick and heal them.

"I have been given all authority in heaven and earth. Therefore go and make disciples in all the nations, baptizing them into the name of the Father and of the Son and of the Holy Spirit, and then teach these new disciples to obey all the commands I have given you; and be sure of this—that I am with you always, even to the end of the world."

Then he said, "When I was with you before, don't you remember my telling you that everything written about me by Moses and the prophets and in the Psalms must all come true?" Then he opened their minds to understand at last these many Scriptures! And he said, "Yes, it was written long ago that the Messiah must suffer and die and rise again from the dead on the third day; and that this message of salvation should be taken from Jerusalem to all the nations: *There is forgiveness of sins for all who turn to me.* You have seen these prophecies come true. And now I will send the Holy Spirit upon you, just as my Father promised. Don't begin telling others yet—stay here in the city until the Holy Spirit comes and fills you with power from heaven."

Matthew 28: 16–20; Mark 16: 15–18; Luke 24: 44–49.

Jesus Is Received into Heaven

Then Jesus led them out along the road to Bethany, and lifting his hands to heaven, he blessed them, and then began rising into the sky, and went on to heaven, and disappeared into a cloud.

They returned to Jerusalem from the Mount of Olives filled with mighty joy. They walked the half mile back to Jerusalem.

They were continually in the Temple, praising God.

Luke 24: 50–53; Luke: Acts 1: 9, 12.

After his crucifixion, Jesus appeared to his chosen apostles, actually alive. In one of these meetings he told them not to leave Jerusalem until the Holy Spirit came upon them in fulfillment of the Father's promise, a matter he had previously discussed with them.

"John baptized you with water," he reminded them, "but you shall be baptized with the Holy Spirit in just a few days."

They asked him, "Lord, are you going to free Israel from Rome now and restore us as an independent nation?"

"The Father sets those dates," he replied, "and they are not for you to know. But when the Holy Spirit has come upon you, you will receive power to testify about me with great effect, to the people in Jerusalem, throughout Judea, in Samaria, and to the ends of the earth, about my death and resurrection."

It was not long afterwards that he rose into the sky, leaving them staring after him.

Luke: Acts 1: 3–9.

15 Later

Paul Persecutes the Christians

Paul was like a wild man, going everywhere to devastate the believers, even entering private homes and dragging out men and women alike and jailing them. Threatening with every breath and eager to destroy every Christian, he went to the High Priest in Jerusalem. He requested a letter addressed to synagogues requiring their cooperation in the persecution of any believers he found, both men and women, so that he could bring them in chains to Jerusalem.

As he was nearing Damascus on this mission, suddenly a brilliant light from heaven spotted down upon him! He fell to the ground and heard a voice saying to him, "Paul! Paul! Why are you persecuting me?"

"Who is speaking, sir?" Paul asked.

And the voice replied, "I am Jesus, the one you are persecuting! Now get up and go into the city and await my further instructions."

The men with Paul stood speechless with surprise, for they heard the sound of someone's voice but saw no one! As Paul picked himself up off the ground, he found that he was blind. He had to be led into Damascus and was there three days, blind, going without food and water all that time.

There was in Damascus a believer named Ananias. The Lord spoke to him in a vision, calling, "Ananias! Go over to Straight Street and find the house of a man named Judas and ask there for Paul of Tarsus. He is praying to me right now, for I have shown him a vision of a man named Ananias coming in and laying his hands on him so that he can see again!"

"But Lord," exclaimed Ananias, "I have heard about the terrible things this man has done to the believers in Jerusalem!"

But the Lord said, "Go and do what I say. For Paul is my chosen instrument to take my message to the nations and before kings, as well as to the people of Israel. And I will show him how much he must suffer for me."

Luke: Acts 8: 3; 9: 1–16.

Paul Becomes A Believer

Ananias found Paul and laid his hands on him and said, "Brother Paul, the Lord Jesus has sent me so that you may be filled with the Holy Spirit and get your sight back." Instantly (it was as though scales fell from his eyes) Paul could see, and was immediately baptized, and went at once to the synagogue to tell everyone there the Good News about Jesus—that he is indeed the Son of God!

Luke: Acts 9: 17–20.

As Peter was saying these things, the Holy Spirit fell upon all those listening! The Jews were amazed that the gift of the Holy Spirit would be given to Gentiles too!

Peter thought of the Lord's words when he said, "Yes, John baptized with water, but you shall be baptized with the Holy Spirit." So he baptized them.

Luke: Acts 10: 44, 45, 48; 11: 16.

The Lord Speaks to Paul

Paul stayed with Titus Justus, a Gentile who worshiped God and lived next door to the synagogue.

One night the Lord spoke to Paul in a vision and told him, "Don't be afraid! Speak out! Don't quit! For I am with you and no one can harm you. Many people here in this city belong to me."

So Paul stayed there the next year and a half, teaching the truths of God.

Luke: Acts 18: 7–11.

The Lord Speaks to Paul

At Miletus, Paul sent a message to the elders of the church at Ephesus to meet him. When they arrived he told them, "You men know that from the day I set foot in Turkey until now I have done the Lord's work humbly, and have faced grave danger from the plots of the Jews against my life. Now I am going to Jerusalem, drawn there irresistibly by the Holy Spirit, not knowing what awaits me. I know that none of you among whom I went about teaching the Kingdom will ever see me again.

"I entrust you to God. I have never been hungry for money or fine clothing. You know that these hands of mine worked to pay my own way. I was a constant example to you in helping the poor; for I remembered the words of the Lord Jesus, 'It is more blessed to give than to receive.'"

When he had finished speaking, he prayed with them, and they wept aloud, sorrowing most of all because he said that he would never see them again. Then they accompanied him down to the ship.

Luke: Acts 20: 17–19, 22, 25, 32–38.

Appendix

Paul's Witness

We went on to Caesarea and stayed at the home of Philip the Evangelist. During our stay of several days, a man named Agabus, who also had the gift of prophecy, arrived from Judea. He took Paul's belt, bound his own feet and hands with it and said, "The Holy Spirit declares, 'So shall the owner of this belt be bound by the Jews in Jerusalem and turned over to the Romans.'" All of us begged Paul not to go on to Jerusalem.

It was clear that he wouldn't be dissuaded. We gave up and left for Jerusalem. The believers at Jerusalem welcomed us cordially. Paul went to the Temple. When some Jews from Turkey saw him in the Temple they roused a mob against him and grabbed him.

Paul was dragged out of the Temple. As they were killing him, the commander of the Roman garrison ordered out his soldiers and officers who ran down among the crowd and arrested him.

Then the commander asked the crowd who he was and what he had done. Some shouted one thing and some another, yelling, "Men of Israel! Help! Help! This is the man who preaches against our people and tells everybody to disobey the Jewish laws. He defies the Temple by bringing Gentiles in!"

Paul said, "I am a Jew, born in Tarsus, a city in Cilicia, but educated here in Jerusalem. I learned to follow our Jewish laws and customs very carefully. I became very anxious to honor God in everything I did. I persecuted the Christians, hounding them to death, binding and delivering both men and women to prison. The High Priest can testify that this is so, for I asked for

Paul's Witness

letters to the Jewish leaders with instructions to let me bring any Christians I found to Jerusalem in chains to be punished.

"As I was on the road, nearing Damascus, suddenly about noon a very bright light from heaven shone around me. And I fell to the ground and heard a voice saying to me, 'Saul, Saul, why are you persecuting me?' 'Who is it speaking to me, sir?' I asked. And he replied, 'I am Jesus of Nazareth, the one you are persecuting.' I said, 'What shall I do, Lord?' And the Lord told me, 'Get up and go into Damascus, and there you will be told what awaits you in the years ahead.'

"I was blinded by the intense light, and had to be led into Damascus by my companions. There a man named Ananias, as godly a man as you could find for obeying the law, came and said, 'Brother Saul, receive your sight!' And that very hour I could see him!

"Then he told me, 'The God of our fathers has chosen you to know his will and to see the Messiah and hear him speak. You are to take his message everywhere, telling what you have seen and heard.'

"After my return to Jerusalem, while I was praying in the Temple, I fell into a trance and saw a vision of God saying to me, 'Hurry! Leave Jerusalem, for the people here won't believe you when you give them my message.' 'But Lord,' I argued, 'they certainly know that I imprisoned and beat those in every synagogue who believed on you. And when your witness Stephen was killed, I was standing there agreeing.' But God said to me, 'Leave Jerusalem, for I will send you far away to the *Gentiles!*'"

The crowd listened until Paul came to that word, then with one voice they shouted, "Away with such a fellow! Kill him! He isn't fit to live!" The commander, fearing they would tear him apart, ordered his soldiers to take him away from them by force and bring him back to the armory.

That night the Lord stood beside Paul and said, "Don't worry, Paul; just as you have told the people about me here in Jerusalem, so you must also in Rome."

The next morning some forty or more of the Jews got together and bound themselves by a curse neither to eat nor drink until they had killed Paul! Paul's nephew got wind of their plan. One of the officers brought the young man to the commander. He told him. The commander called two of his officers and ordered, "Get 200 soldiers ready to leave for Caesarea at nine o'clock tonight! Take 200 spearmen and 70 mounted cavalry. Give Paul a horse to ride and get him safely to Governor Felix. Then he wrote this letter to the governor: "This man was seized by the Jews and they were killing him when I sent the soldiers to rescue him, for I learned that he was a Roman citizen."

When the cavalry arrived in Caesarea, they presented Paul and the letter to the governor. The governor ordered him kept in the prison at King Herod's palace.

A few days later Felix, the governor, sent for Paul and listened as Paul reasoned about righteousness and self-control and the judgment to come. Felix was terrified. "Go away for now," he replied, "and when I have a more convenient time, I'll call for you again."

Two years went by in this way; then Felix was succeeded by Porcius Festus. And because Felix wanted to gain favor with the Jews, he left Paul in chains. Festus, anxious to please the Jews, asked Paul, "Are you willing to go to Jerusalem and stand trial before me?"

But Paul replied, "No! I demand my privilege of a hearing before the Emperor himself. You know very well I am not guilty. If I have done something worthy of death, I don't refuse to die! But if I am innocent, neither you nor anyone else has a right to turn me over to these men to kill me. *I appeal to Caesar.*"

A few days later King Agrippa arrived for a visit with Festus. Festus discussed Paul's case with the king. "There is a prisoner here," he told him, "whose case was left for me by Felix. When I was in Jerusalem, the chief priests and other Jewish leaders gave me their side of the story and asked me to have him killed. Of course I quickly pointed out to them that Roman law does not convict a man before he is tried. He is given an opportunity to defend himself face to face with his accusers. But Paul appealed to Caesar!"

Paul's Great Speech Before King Agrippa

"I'd like to hear the man myself," Agrippa said.

The next day, after the king had arrived at the courtroom with great pomp, accompanied by military officers and prominent men of the city, Festus ordered Paul brought in. Festus addressed King Agrippa: "This is the man whose death is demanded by the Jews. But in my opinion he has done nothing worthy of death. However he appealed his case to Caesar, and I have no alternative but to send him. But what shall I write the Emperor? For there is no real charge against him! So I have brought him before you, King Agrippa, to examine him and then tell me what to write."

Luke: Acts (parts of) Chapters 21, 22, 23, 24, 25.

Paul's Great Speech Before King Agrippa

Agrippa said to Paul, "Go ahead. Tell us your story." So Paul presented his defense:

"I am fortunate, King Agrippa," he began, "to be able to present my answer before you, for I know you are an expert on Jewish laws and customs. Now please listen patiently!

"As the Jews are well aware, I was given a thorough Jewish training from my earliest childhood in Tarsus and later at Jerusalem, and I lived accordingly. If they would admit it, they know that I have always been the strictest of Pharisees when it comes to obedience to Jewish laws and customs. But the real reason behind their accusations is something else—it is because I am looking forward to the fulfillment of God's promise made to our ancestors. The twelve tribes of Israel strive night and day to attain this same hope I have! Yet, O King, for me it is a crime, they say! But is it a crime to believe in the resurrection of the dead? Does it seem incredible to you that God can bring men back to life again?

"I used to believe that I ought to do many horrible things to the followers of Jesus of Nazareth. I imprisoned many of the saints in Jerusalem, as authorized by the High Priests; and when they were condemned to death, I cast my vote against them. I used torture to try to make Christians everywhere curse Christ.

I was so violently opposed to them that I even hounded them in distant cities in foreign lands.

"I was on such a mission to Damascus, armed with the authority and commission of the chief priests, when one day about noon, sir, a light from heaven brighter than the sun shone down on me. We all fell down, and I heard a voice speaking to me in Hebrew, 'Saul, Saul, why are you persecuting me? You are only hurting yourself.'

"Who are you, sir?" I asked.

"And the Lord replied, 'I am Jesus, the one you are persecuting. Now stand up! For I have appeared to you to appoint you as my servant and my witness. You are to tell the world about this experience and about the many other occasions when I shall appear to you. And I will protect you from both your own people and the Gentiles. Yes, I am going to send you to the Gentiles to open their eyes to their true condition so that they may repent and live in the light of God instead of in Satan's darkness; so that they may receive forgiveness for their sins and God's inheritance along with all people everywhere whose sins are cleansed away, who are set apart by faith in me.'

"And so, O King Agrippa, I was not disobedient to that vision from heaven! I preached first to those in Damascus, then in Jerusalem and through Judea, and also to the Gentiles that all must forsake their sins and turn to God—and prove their repentance by doing good deeds. The Jews arrested me in the Temple for preaching this, and tried to kill me, but God protected me so that I am still alive today to tell these facts to everyone, both great and small. I teach nothing except what the prophets and Moses said—that the Messiah would suffer, and be the First to rise from the dead, to bring light to Jews and Gentiles alike."

Suddenly Festus shouted, "Paul, you are insane. Your long studying has broken your mind!"

But Paul replied, "I am not insane, Most Excellent Festus. I speak words of sober truth. And King Agrippa knows about these things. I speak frankly for I am sure these events are all familiar to him, for they were not done in a corner! King

Agrippa, do you believe the prophets? But I know you do—"

Agrippa interrupted him. "With trivial proofs like these, you expect me to become a Christian?"

And Paul replied, "Would to God that whether my arguments are trivial or strong, both you and everyone here in this audience might become the same as I am, except for these chains."

Agrippa said to Festus, "He could be set free if he hadn't appealed to Caesar!"

Luke: Acts 26: 1–32.

Arrangements were finally made to start us on our way to Rome by ship; so Paul and several other prisoners were placed in the custody of an officer named Julius, a member of the imperial guard. We left on a boat which was scheduled to make several stops along the Turkish coast.

The next day we docked at Sidon. Putting to sea from there, we encountered headwinds that made it difficult to keep the ship on course, so we sailed north of Cyprus, landing at Myra, in the province of Lycia. There our officer found an Egyptian ship from Alexandria, bound for Italy, and put us aboard.

Luke: Acts 27: 1–6.

Strength is Made Perfect in Weakness

I was given a physical condition which has been a thorn in my flesh, a messenger from Satan to hurt and bother me, and prick my pride. Three different times I begged God to make me well again.

Each time he said, "No. But I am with you; that is all you need. My power shows up best in weak people."

Paul: II Corinthians 12: 7–9.

Heard by John in Visions

God permitted Jesus Christ to reveal future things to his servant John. John wrote it all down—the words of God and Jesus Christ and everything he heard and saw.

If you read this prophecy aloud to the church, you will receive a special blessing from the Lord. Those who listen to it being read and do what it says will also be blessed. For the time is near when these things will all come true.

It was the Lord's Day and I, John, was worshiping, when suddenly I heard a loud voice behind me, a voice that sounded like a trumpet blast, saying, "I am A and Z, the First and Last!" And then I heard him say, "Write down everything you see, and send your letter to the seven churches in Turkey; to the church in Ephesus, the one in Smyrna, and those in Pergamos, Thyatira, Sardis, Philadelphia, and Laodicea."

When I turned to see who was speaking, there behind me were seven candlesticks of gold. And standing among them was one who looked like Jesus who called himself the Son of Man, wearing a long robe circled with a golden band across his chest. His hair was white as wool or snow, and his eyes penetrated like flames of fire. His feet gleamed like burnished bronze, and his voice thundered like the waves against the shore. He held seven stars in his right hand and a sharp, double-bladed sword in his mouth, and his face shone like the power of the sun in unclouded brilliance.

When I saw him, I fell at his feet as dead; but he laid his right hand on me and said, "Don't be afraid! I am the First and the Last, the Living One who died, who is now alive forevermore, who has the keys of hell and death—don't be afraid! Write down what you have just seen, and what will soon be shown to you.

"This is the meaning of the seven stars you saw in my right hand, and the seven golden candlesticks: The seven stars are the leaders of the seven churches, and the seven candlesticks are the churches themselves."

Revelation 1: 1–3; 9–20.

Messages to the Churches

"Write a letter to the leader of the church at Ephesus and tell him this:

"I write to inform you of a message from him who walks among the churches and holds their leaders in his right hand.

Messages to the Churches

"He says to you: I know how many good things you are doing. I have watched your hard work and your patience; I know you don't tolerate sin among your members, and you have carefully examined the claims of those who say they are apostles but aren't. You have found out how they lie. You have patiently suffered for me without quitting.

"Yet there is one thing wrong; you don't love me as at first! Think about those times of your first love (how different now!) and turn back to me again and work as you did before; or else I will come and remove your candlestick from its place among the churches.

"But there is this about you that is good: You hate the deeds of the licentious Nicolaitans, just as I do.

"Let this message sink into the ears of anyone who listens to what the Spirit is saying to the churches: To everyone who is victorious, I will give fruit from the Tree of Life in the Paradise of God."

Revelation 2: 1–7.

"To the leader of the church in Smyrna write this letter:
"This message is from him who is the First and Last, who was dead and then came back to life.

"I know how much you suffer for the Lord, and I know all about your poverty (but you have heavenly riches!). I know the slander of those opposing you, who say that they are Jews—the children of God—but they aren't, for they support the cause of Satan. Stop being afraid of what you are about to suffer—for the devil will soon throw some of you into prison to test you. You will be persecuted for 'ten days.' Remain faithful even when facing death and I will give you the crown of life—an unending, glorious future. Let everyone who can hear, listen to what the Spirit is saying to the churches: He who is victorious shall not be hurt by the Second Death."

Revelation 2: 8–11.

"Write this letter to the leader of the church in Pergamos:
"This message is from him who wields the sharp and double-

bladed sword. I am fully aware that you live in the city where Satan's throne is, at the center of satanic worship; and yet you have remained loyal to me, and refused to deny me, even when Antipas, my faithful witness, was martyred among you by Satan's devotees.

"And yet I have a few things against you. You tolerate some among you who do as Balaam did when he taught Balak how to ruin the people of Israel by involving them in sexual sin and encouraging them to go to idol feasts. Yes, you have some of these very same followers of Balaam among you!

"Change your mind and attitude, or else I will come to you suddenly and fight against them with the sword of my mouth.

"Let everyone who can hear, listen to what the Spirit is saying to the churches: Every one who is victorious shall eat of the hidden manna, the secret nourishment from heaven; and I will give to each a white stone, and on the stone will be engraved a new name that no one else knows except the one receiving it."

Revelation 2: 12–17.

"Write this letter to the leader of the church in Thyatira:

"This is a message from the Son of God, whose eyes penetrate like flames of fire, whose feet are like glowing brass.

"I am aware of all your good deeds—your kindness to the poor, your gifts and service to them; also I know your love and faith and patience, and I can see your constant improvement in all these things.

"Yet I have this against you: You are permitting that woman Jezebel, who calls herself a prophetess, to teach my servants that sex sin is not a serious matter; she urges them to practice immorality and to eat meat that has been sacrificed to idols. I gave her time to change her mind and attitude, but she refused. Pay attention now to what I am saying: I will lay her upon a sickbed of intense affliction, along with all her immoral followers, unless they turn again to me, repenting of their sin with her; and I will strike her children dead. And all the churches shall know that I am he who searches deep within men's hearts, and minds; I will give to each of you whatever you deserve.

Messages to the Churches

"As for the rest of you in Thyatira who have not followed this false teaching ('deeper truths,' as they call them—depths of Satan, really), I will ask nothing further of you; only hold tightly to what you have until I come.

"To every one who overcomes—who to the very end keeps on doing things that please me—I will give power over the nations. You will rule them with a rod of iron just as my Father gave me the authority to rule them; they will be shattered like a pot of clay that is broken into tiny pieces. And I will give you the Morning Star!

"Let all who can hear, listen to what the Spirit says to the churches."

Revelation 2: 18–29.

"To the leader of the church in Sardis write this letter:

"This message is sent to you by the one who has the seven-fold Spirit of God and the seven stars.

"I know your reputation as a live and active church, but you are dead. Now wake up! Strengthen what little remains—for even what is left is at the point of death. Your deeds are far from right in the sight of God. Go back to what you heard and believed at first; hold to it firmly and turn to me again. Unless you do, I will come suddenly upon you, unexpected as a thief, and punish you.

"Yet even there in Sardis some haven't soiled their garments with the world's filth; they shall walk with me in white, for they are worthy. Everyone who conquers will be clothed in white, and I will not erase his name from the Book of Life, but I will announce before my Father and his angels that he is mine.

"Let all who can hear, listen to what the Spirit is saying to the churches."

Revelation 3: 1–6.

"Write this letter to the leader of the church in Philadelphia:

"This message is sent to you by the one who is holy and true, and has the key of David to open what no one can shut and to shut what no one can open.

"I know you well; you aren't strong, but you have tried to obey and have not denied my Name. Therefore, I have opened a door to you that no one can shut.

"Note this: I will force those supporting the causes of Satan while claiming to be mine (but they aren't—they are lying) to fall at your feet and acknowledge that you are the ones I love.

"Because you have patiently obeyed me, despite the persecution, therefore I will protect you from the time of Great Tribulation and temptation, which will come upon the world to test everyone alive. Look, I am coming soon! Hold tightly to the little strength you have—so that no one will take away your crown.

"As for the one who conquers, I will make him a pillar in the temple of my God; he will be secure, and will go out no more; and I will write my God's Name on him, and he will be a citizen in the city of my God—the New Jerusalem, coming down from heaven from my God; and he will have my new Name inscribed upon him.

"Let all who can hear, listen to what the Spirit is saying to the churches."

Revelation 3: 7–13.

"Write this letter to the leader of the church in Laodicea:
"This message is from the one who stands firm, the faithful and true Witness of all that is or was or evermore shall be, the primeval source of God's creation.

"I know you well—you are neither hot nor cold; I wish you were one or the other! But since you are merely lukewarm, I will spit you out of my mouth!

"You say, 'I am rich, with everything I want; I don't need a thing!' And you don't realize that spiritually you are wretched and miserable and poor and blind and naked.

"My advice to you is to buy pure gold from me, gold purified by fire—only then will you truly be rich. And to purchase from me white garments, clean and pure, so you won't be naked and ashamed; and to get medicine from me to heal your eyes and give you back your sight. I continually discipline and punish everyone I love; so I must punish you, unless you turn from your indifference and become enthusiastic about the things of God.

"Look! I have been standing at the door and I am constantly knocking. If anyone hears me calling him and opens the door, I will come in and fellowship with him and he with me. I will let every one who conquers sit beside me on my throne, just as I took my place with my Father on his throne when I had conquered. Let those who can hear, listen to what the Spirit is saying to the churches."

Revelation 3: 14–22.

Blessed are the Dead Who Die in the Lord

Then as I looked, I saw a door standing open in heaven, and the same voice I had heard before, that sounded like a mighty trumpet blast, spoke to me and said, "Come up here and I will show you what must happen in the future!"

And instantly I was, in spirit, there in heaven and saw—oh, the glory of it!—a throne and someone sitting on it!

And I heard a voice in the heavens above me saying, "Write this down: At last the time has come for his martyrs to enter into their full reward. Yes, says the Spirit, they are blest indeed, for now they shall rest from all their toils and trials; for their good deeds follow them to heaven!

"Take note: I will come as unexpectedly as a thief! Blessed are all who are awaiting me, who keep their robes in readiness and will not need to walk naked and ashamed."

And the angel dictated this sentence to me: "Blessed are those who are invited to the wedding feast of the Lamb." And he added, "God himself has stated this."

Then I fell down at his feet to worship him, but he said, "No! Don't! For I am a servant of God just as you are, and as your brother Christians are, who testify of their faith in Jesus. The purpose of all prophecy and of all I have shown you is to tell about Jesus."

And the one sitting on the throne said, "See, I am making all things new!" And then he said to me, "Write this down, for what I tell you is trustworthy and true:"

Revelation 4: 1–2; 14: 13; 16: 15; 19: 9, 10; 21: 5.

The Fountain of the Water of Life

"It is finished! I am the A and the Z—the Beginning and the End. I will give to the thirsty the springs of the Water of Life —as a gift! Everyone who conquers will inherit all these blessings, and I will be his God and he will be my son. But cowards who turn back from following me, and those who are unfaithful to me, and the corrupt, and murderers, and the immoral, and those conversing with demons, and idol worshipers and all liars —their doom is in the Lake that burns with fire and sulphur. This is the Second Death."

Then the angel said to me, "These words are trustworthy and true: 'I am coming soon!' God, who tells his prophets what the future holds, has sent his angel to tell you this will happen soon. Blessed are those who believe it and all else written in the scroll."

I, John, saw and heard all these things, and fell down to worship the angel who showed them to me; but again he said, "No, don't do anything like that. I, too, am a servant of Jesus as you are, and as your brothers the prophets are, as well as all those who heed the truth stated in this Book. Worship God alone."

Then he instructed me, "Do not seal up what you have written, for the time of fulfillment is near. And when that time comes, all doing wrong will do it more and more; the vile will become more vile; good men will be better; those who are holy will continue on in greater holiness.

"See, I am coming soon, and my reward is with me, to repay everyone according to the deeds he has done. I am the A and the Z, the Beginning and the End, the First and Last. Blessed forever are all who are washing their robes, to have the right

The Fountain of the Water of Life

to enter in through the gates of the city, and to eat the fruit from the Tree of Life.

"Outside the city are those who have strayed away from God, and the sorcerers and the immoral and murderers and idolaters, and all who love to lie, and do so. I, Jesus, have sent my angel to you to tell the churches all these things. I am both David's Root and his Descendant. I am the bright Morning Star. The Spirit and the bride say, 'Come.' Let each one who hears them say the same, 'Come.' Let the thirsty one come—anyone who wants to; let him come and drink the Water of Life without charge.

"And I solemnly declare to everyone who reads this book: If anyone adds anything to what is written here, God shall add to him the plagues described in this book. And if anyone subtracts any part of these prophecies, God shall take away his share in the Tree of Life, and in the Holy City just described.

"He who has said all these things declares: Yes, I am coming soon!"

Amen! Come, Lord Jesus!

The grace of our Lord Jesus Christ be with you all. Amen!

Revelations 21: 6–8; 22: 6–21.